MICHELANGELO AND RAPHAEL

WITH BOTTICELLI - PERUGINO SIGNORELLI - GHIRLANDAIO AND ROSSELLI

IN THE VATICAN

ALL THE SISTINE CHAPEL, THE STANZAS AND THE LOGGIAS

Special Edition for the Museums and Papal Galleries

THE SISTINE CHAPEL

The Sistine Chapel takes its name from Pope Sixtus IV Della Rovere. According to Vasari, he commissioned the Florentine Baccio Pontelli in 1475 to design a building that would house the palace chapel and also serve as a Vatican fortress (the crenelation of the battlements continues to testify to this second purpose). The actual construction was left to Giovannino de' Dolci – often mentioned in contemporary Vatican documents – who also supervised the pictorial decorations in the chapel until its formal inauguration on August 15, 1483. Designer and builder are both immortalized with portraits in Perugino's fresco, *Jesus Handing the Keys to St. Peter*, on the Sistine Chapel wall.

The interior of the chapel consists of a single long nave (13,41 x 40,23 meters) surmounted by a flattened barrel vault with spandrels and a lunette above each of the twelve arched windows. The floor is of multicolored marble. A high marble chancel screen separates the presbytery from the general body of the chapel. The chancel screen and the choir stalls, decorated in delicate ornamental relief, are the work of Mino da Fiesole and his assistants. The dimensions of the chapel, corresponding exactly to those of the Jerusalem Temple; the division between presbytery and body of the chapel; the original paintings – all these features testify to the Pope's desire to fashion a Renaissance version of the great Roman basilicas, with close ties however to the paleochristian and medieval traditions of the Catholic Church.

DECORATION OF THE WALLS

The original paintings, executed by a large group of Tuscan and Umbrian artists, make up a band of frescoes representing two great cycles from the Old and the New Testament. The scenes were placed in symbolic correspondence in a high band that ran just below the height of the windows along all the walls. Below these, a stretch of simulated draperies framed a series of Della Rovere family crests. Only a fragment of this work still remains on the left lateral wall near the entrance. The remainder was painted over in the 19th century. A series of portraits of the first thirty popes was set high between the windows. Of this work, done between 1480 and 1483, only the part on the lateral walls was preserved. In order to make way for Michelangelo's *Last Judgment* on the altar wall, the originals were destroyed; the paintings on the entrance wall were redone after the architrave of the Sala Regia door collapsed in the first half of the 16th century.

The Life of Moses

Originally, this biblical cycle consisted of eight scenes: six on the left lateral wall and two on the end walls. The first scene, in the left side of the altar wall, was done by Perugino and, as mentioned above, later destroyed. It represented the *Finding of Moses* and corresponded to the *Birth of Christ* on the right side. In the center, a panel represented the *Assumption of Our Lady* (to whom the chapel is consecrated) *Venerated by Sixtus IV*.

On the left wall, starting at the altar, the existing frescoes begin with the *Journey of Moses into Egypt*, a synthesis grouping several episodes into a single scene – a common enough medieval practice. We see Moses taking leave of his father-in-law; his return to Egypt; the circumcision of the second-born. The last episode is unimportant in itself but serves to balance and correspond to the *Baptism of Christ in the Jordan* in the cycle on the life of Christ. The Moses painting, not of exceptional quality, was done by Perugino to whom the overall design and most of the portraits are also attributed. The rest was executed by his most talented pupil, Pinturicchio, who was also the author of the lovely landscape, soft and shaded in the Umbrian manner.

The second painting shows several scenes from the *Life of Moses* (Moses slays the Egyptian; Moses puts the shepherds to flight; his vision of God in the burning bush on Mount Horeb) centered around the meeting of Moses with the *Daughters of Jethro*, one of whom becomes his wife. This painting ranks as one of Botticelli's masterpieces. He gave the central episode, executed with the graphic elegance and subtle musical rhythm that characterizes all his work, a mood of melancholy meditation on the frailty of beauty; and he re-echoed the mood in the romantic wooded landscape.

Cosimo Rosselli, one of the less gifted of the Sistine Chapel artists, did the *Crossing of the Red Sea*. The contrast between the Hebrews – bathed in a soft sunlight – and the Egyptians – under the harsh clouds of an impending storm – simply lacks subtlety. The most interesting parts of the painting are the portraits done by Piero di Cosimo. Particularly notable is the portrait of Cardinal Bessarione, in priest's soutane, carrying a reliquary. The appearance of this figure gives the episode a « contemporary » symbolic meaning by suggesting the Crusades which this high prelate heatedly supported.

Again by Cosimo Rosselli, who was helped by Piero di Cosimo, is the fourth painting relating to the story of the *Ten Commandments*. The different episodes (Moses ascends Mount Sinai; the adoration of the golden calf; the punishment of the idolatrous Hebrews; the second vision on Mount Sinai; Moses descends with the Ten Commandments), overlap each other creating an effect of confusion and complexity.

The *Punishment of Korah, Dathan, and Abiram* – Hebrew priests who denied the religious and civil authority of Moses and Aaron over the Hebrew people – is an extremely fascinating work by Botticelli (whose self-portrait is the second figure from the right). The scene shows Korah, Dathan, and Abiram plus their families swallowed by the earth. The composition is cleverly done, contrasting the calm serenity of Moses and Aaron and the convulsive movements of the punished rebels. It takes place against an urban background in which such Roman monuments as the Arch of Constantine and the (now destroyed) Settizonio stand out prominently. An element of great documentary significance, rarely depicted in biblical iconography, it is meant to confirm the authority of the Popes conferred upon them by God. This intention is again emphasized in the corresponding painting on the opposite wall, *Jesus Handing over the Keys to St. Peter*, the first Pope.

The last painting on the left wall shows *Moses Reading His Last Testament to His People*. It too tells several stories: the testament of Moses in the presence of Joshua and a youth of the tribe of Levi; Moses sees the promised land from Mount Nebo; the death of Moses. Although Signorelli was very young at the time he did this painting, the same plastic quality and bold graphic design that were to characterize his later work are already in evidence. The figure of his young nude must have had considerable influence on Michelangelo when the latter worked on the chapel ceiling. This painting includes several portraits of unidentified cotnemporary personalities.

The cycle was concluded with Signorelli's *Contest over the Body of Moses* on the entrance wall. When this wall collapsed, the painting went with it. On the new wall, during the reign of Gregory VII, Matteo da Lecce did a rather mediocre fresco, on the same subject, in the late-mannered style.

The Life of Christ

Originally, this cycle also included eight scenes. On the right side of the end wall, Perugino did a *Birth of Christ* which was destroyed to make room for the *Last Judgment*. On the right lateral wall, we begin with the *Baptism of Christ in the Jordan*. Perugino's signature was recently discovered on it; judging however by the mediocre quality of the painting, we must assume that it was more likely – and in great measure – done by his assistants.

The second painting, the *Purification of the Leper*, was done by Botticelli in minute biblical detail. The episode, of no great significance in itself – particularly when compared with the *Temptation of Christ* which was relegated to the back – takes on special meaning when one recalls that Sixtus IV once wrote a treatise (« De Sanguine Christi ») on the cleansing value of the Blood of Sacrifice and sponsored various initiatives to care for the sick and invalid. He founded the still existing and functioning Santo Spirito Hospital – which appears in the background of this painting in the guise of the Temple of Jerusalem. In spite of Botticelli's unquestionably high talent for composition, this work is not among his best: all those symbolic allusions, extraneous to the episode itself, weigh it down unnecessarily.

The next two paintings are no better and are interesting above all for their numerous portraits and vast landscapes. The *Vocation of the Apostles*, by Ghirlandaio, depicts two scenes: the call of Peter and Andrew – both shown at work in their boat – and of James and John – intent on mending their nets. The presence of the large crowd in the background is a rather disturbing element: its only purpose seems to be to add those elegant figures and contemporary portraits to an otherwise static picture. The paintings of the *Sermon on the Mount and the Healing of the Leper* by Cosimo Rosselli have too many descriptive details. Only the highly imaginative and dramatically monumental landscapes of Piero di Cosimo stand out.

Recognized as one of the masterpieces of the Sistine Chapel is the magnificently beautiful fifth painting on this side: *Jesus Hands over the Keys to St. Peter*. Painted by Perugino, it was almost entirely executed by him (except for some of the secondary figures among whom Baccio Pontelli and Giovannino de' Dolci – probably done by Signorelli). The scene centers around the group with Christ who hands the keys to Peter kneeling before him. The keys are gold – symbol of the « power of judging » granted to the Popes – and silver – symbol of the « power of discerning. » On either side, the Apostles and several onlookers form two converging lines with their slow, majestic procession. In the background, two symmetrical views of the Arch of Constantine frame the Temple of Jerusalem – a huge octagonal building surmounted by a dome that suggests the coming architecture of the 16th century beginning with Bramante. The wide open space all around the figures suggests an atmosphere of solemn peace in which Christ transfers his powers to Peter, his vicar on earth.

The final scene on this wall is the *Last Supper*. The setting for it is a many-sided hall with three windows. Through these, we see the three key episodes of the Passion: Christ's prayer in Gethsemane, the kiss of Judas, and the Crucifixion. For clarity of composition, keen perspective, and the dignified solemnity of the figures, this surely is Cosimo Rosselli's masterpiece. He rightly takes his place among the great artists of the Tuscan school.

The cycle was concluded on the entrance wall with the *Resurrection of Christ* by Ghirlandaio. After its destruction, another painting on the same subject by the mannerist Hendrijk van den Broeck (Arrigo Paludano) replaced it.

The Series of Pontiffs

Set between the windows in elegant Renaissance niches, the portraits of the Roman pontiffs provided a decorative complement once typical in old Roman churches, but abandoned for some time. In the Sistine Chapel, these works are not of high quality although some are attributed to unquestionably high talent (eight to Ghirlandaio; seven to Botticelli; two to Rosselli; and seven to Fra' Diamante). Twenty-seven are still in place, but four others (Christ and the first three Popes) were once on the altar wall and therefore were destroyed to make room for the *Last Judgment*.

Iconographic Interpretation

We mentioned above that the cycles of Moses and of Christ are closely balanced: Moses – who freed the Chosen People from slavery in Egypt – prefigures Christ – who freed all mankind from the slavery of sin. At times, the correspondence is obvious, particularly when single episodes are contrasted on opposite walls. But this is not always the case. We receive help from the Latin inscriptions (recently discovered during the work of renovation) which run just above the paintings. The inscriptions were published in 1513 in a printed notice on the occasion of the conclave that followed the death of Julius II. With the help of the Latin inscriptions, the plan of Sixtus IV is very clear. He wanted to reaffirm, in strict theological precision, the close correspondence existing between the Old and the New Testament, between the Kingdom of Law and the Kingdom of Grace. The series of Pontiffs logically belongs within this framework for they are the successors and vicars of Christ just as Moses was his precursor. In other words, ideally there is an unbroken continuty in the life of mankind before, during, and after the Redemption; and this continuity is ensured even now by the presence of the Popes.

This then is the ideology, inspired by medieval Catholicism and theocratic doctrine, of the wall decorations. It was far from pure chance that guided Sixtus IV in his general plan and in his selection of specific narratives (for example, uniting events historically separated in time) from the old Roman basilicas. Insisting on his scheme imposed a heavy burden on artists formed under the new ideology of the Renaissance. Little wonder therefore that the Pope's favorites were not the ardent revolutionaries like Signorelli and Piero di Cosimo, but rather the modest and retiring Rosselli and Ghirlandaio or those who were willing to compromise, like Perugino. In fine, it must be admitted that this single-minded determination which subjected the will and personal style of several artists, this single point of view making the work of many artists one integrated whole, resulted in one of the greatest accomplishments of all the Italian « Quattrocento. »

THE CEILING

In March, 1508, Pope Julius II called on Michelangelo to paint the Sistine Chapel ceiling which originally was blue with gold stars. Michelangelo accepted the commission even though he considered himself more sculptor than painter and preferred devoting his time to the monumental tomb of Julius II started in 1505. The Pope deserves praise for his choice; this artist, relatively inexperienced in painting, became the ideal interpreter for the grand undertaking.

Vasari reports the rumor, malicious but probably true, that Bramante had something to do with the Pope's choice. He thereby hoped to impede work on the

Julius II tomb and damage the reputation of Michelangelo who was his and Raphael's open rival. Buonarroti loudly declined the Pope's call at first and it was only at the latter's repeated insistence that he finally set to work in May, 1508. He carried on the task by himself, refusing even the help of laborers, while immersed in a thousand technical difficulties about which he writes in charming letters still extant. The work proceded rapidly in spite of the difficulties. The first part of the ceiling was unveiled in August of 1511, and the solemn inauguration, with Julius II presiding, took place on November 2, 1512.

The original plan included twelve heroic-sized Apostles. Michelangelo even made preliminary sketches for them (now in the British Museum). However, as we read in his letter of 1524 to his friend Fattucci, he soon changed the plan. The complete execution, therefore – the structural design as well as the pictorial and ideological themes – was Michelangelo's alone.

The vast expanse of the ceiling shows up as a single coherent pattern made up of harmoniously flowing parts. No optical illusion is intended; instead, the painted architectonic designs serve to frame and re-enforce the scenes. Vasari remarked that « there is no static view. » He meant, of course, that there is not just one single spot from which the viewer should admire this or that scene; there are many viewing points arranged in chronological succession depending on the spectator's position and time of viewing. Above the main structural cornice is the lower area of the ceiling with spandrels and lunettes holding the « Ancestors of Christ » (except the corner spandrels which contain four « Miraculous Salvations of Israel »). In the upper part of this area, the run of corbels is decorated with « putti » in monochrome. The corbels define the intermediate area – that of the Prophets and Sibyls – and also support a robust painted cornice which is actually parallel (but appears higher) to the chapel walls. Finally, the cornice is connected by large bands to the pilasters on both sides of the thrones forming the frames for the nine scenes from Genesis arranged in sequence in the central area of the ceiling. Each of the colossal « Ignudi » (nudes) is seated on one of the twenty blocks surmounting the pilasters.

Another feature binding the various elements is the pictorial plan with its own intrinsic logic yet innocent of any specific philosophical system. The Neoplatonism to which Buonarroti was privy in Medici Florence and the Franciscan theory of the « Tree of Life » should not be insisted upon here even though the artist's broad cultural and spiritual formation undoubtedly included them. The heart of the narrative is the biblical texts from Genesis elaborated by Michelangelo as the myth of the Origin of Man. The validity of this theme today and for all time is suggested by the presence of the « Ignudi » who participate in the drama like the quiet, watchful chorus in a Greek tragedy. Beyond their literal meaning as part of the history of salvation, scenes are employed to reveal the state of man's soul after sin: sadness of uncertain expectation (ancestors of Christ); blind hope of a miracle (salvation of Israel); the profound serenity from knowledge of the future (the Prophets and Sibyls). Looking at it this way, we see the pattern on the ceiling as one gigantic spiritual history of mankind.

Histories from Genesis

The nine episodes are ideally divided into three groups relating to the origins of Universe, of Man, of Evil. In the first group (*Division of Light from*

Darkness, Creation of the Sun and the Moon, Dividing the Waters from the Land and the Creation of the Animals), God is the sole protagonist. He appears alone and solemn in the empty sky, and yet bursting with the energy which will erupt into a sudden, violent act of creation. In the second group, the figure of man appears fragile and naked in contrast to the massive might of the figure of the Father. Adam, painfully awakened from the torpor of unconsciousness, is snatched into life as if by a magnetic force; Eve responds to the sound of the divine command and assumes a prayerful attitude. In the *Fall and the Expulsion*, the inescapable connection between sin and punishment is thrust upon us by the fusion of the two episodes into one, divided and nevertheless joined, by the fearsome apparition of the serpent. The high dramatic moment of Sin passes from the barren landscape into an eternal dimension. Mankind is the protagonist in the third grouping as the composition becomes crowded, not unlike a choral drama. We admire the calm serenity of the *Sacrifice of Noah* as it contrasts with the dramatic agitation of the *Deluge*, that nameless cataclysm engulfing masses of humanity into terror and anguish. The cycle concludes with the *Drunkenness of Noah*, symbol of man saved from danger but ineluctably slave to sin.

The Ignudi

The colossal nudes are one of the most mysterious and ingenious creations of Michelangelo's spirituality. In their heroic nudity the artist saw the purity of man created in the image and likeness of God. They express intense vitality ranging from mute contemplation to crying despair, from melancholy resignation to mad terror. They sum up mankind reacting with all the sinews of its being to the mystery of man slave to sin. They mediate between God and man; they join the myth to the present moment in a meditation that knows no time.

The Prophets and Sibyls

Immediately below the large simulated cornice on the ceiling's middle area, on huge thrones framed by painted columns, sit the Prophets and Sibyls. They alternate on the lateral walls, whereas each of the end walls has only the figure of a Prophet. The ornamental scrolls identify them. Beginning from the back and moving to the right, we find: *Jonah*, in a state of ecstasy at the vision of God; the *Sibyl of Lybia* gently turning toward the open book; *Daniel*, a beardless youth, intent upon transcribing what he finds in the giant book; the *Cumaean Sibyl*, face lined with age, absorbed in meditation; *Isaiah* caught in a moment of reverie as he turns his noble head; the *Delphic Sibyl* with limpid, wide-open eyes straining into the void; *Zechariah*, a dignified bearded man attentively studying a book; *Joel*, face matured through long spiritual effort; the *Eritrean Sibyl*, youthful, serene, about to open her book; the aged, turbanned *Ezekiel* staring at the youth beside him; the *Persian Sibyl* immersed in her reading, her worn features mocked by the harsh light; *Jeremiah*, bearded chin resting in his hand, deep in pensive contemplation of sorrow. Each of these magnificent figures is surrounded by one or more of the genii – the putti – who sometimes participate in the action or, more often, bear witness to the prophet's presence. By their various attitudes, they give testimony to the unceasing hope of redemption of mankind.

Both the Prophets and Sibyls see into the future: they represent that part of mankind which believes in the Messiah and which transmits its hope in his coming to future generations. It should be noted that while the Prophets in fact foretold the coming of the Messiah to the chosen people, the Sibyls belong to the pagan world. The parallel therefore is superficial, based on their divining gifts. We see nevertheless that in the larger context of Michelangelo's spirituality, the expectation of redemption does not – and cannot – belong exclusively to one people. It must involve all of mankind.

The Ancestors of Christ and the Salvations of Israel

Not as well-known, but not less artistically coherent nor less pictorially important is the series of the « Ancestors of Christ » in the eight spandrels (invariably family groups of three figures) and in the lunettes between spandrels and the Prophets and Sibyls. These groups serve a double function. On the one hand they point to the coming of the Messiah as an historical continuity and reveal the divine plan for redemption as early as the moment of sin. On the other hand, their wild, terror-filled expressions and their evident pain reveal the sad state of the human condition after sin – ignorant of a salvation they cannot imagine. Thus, they represent an alternative to the Prophets who draw their strength from the conviction of an inevitable redemption.

The cycle concludes with the corner spandrels containing episodes in which the Hebrew people were saved by divine intervention: the *Punishment of Haman*, the *Brazen Serpent*, *Judith and Holophernes*, and *David and Goliath*. These frescoes have a specific pictorial purpose, for they serve as a link to the paintings below them (the Life of Moses). They prefigure the coming of the Messiah: they underscore the continuous presence of God in the life of his people and the constant renewal of his promise of redemption through the miraculous actions in dramatically desperate circumstances.

We mentioned earlier that Michelangelo worked alone, without help of any kind, even for the menial tasks. The stylistic variations that can be detected should be attributed therefore to his spiritual and artistic growth. When he began the monumental undertaking he had no great expertise in painting technique. True, he already painted such important works as the *Tondo Doni* and the cartoon for the *Battle of Cascina*, but a challenge in fresco was entirely new to him. He was – and wished to be considered – a sculptor; the mentality of a painter was not his. To him, a painted image meant transcription of a sculptured image on a flat surface; everything, in other words, reduced to the bare values of drawing and chiaroscuro. This explains why, in the early frescoes (the Noah scenes), the figures seem carved in the round by sheer force of design. Colors here play only a secondary role and the compositions are crowded as if the artist « feared a vacuum, » but really because he did not yet master the feeling for open space. Having later mastered the technique (the creation of man, the Ignudi, the Prophets and Sibyls), he also mastered composition: the figures, isolated yet animated, radiate vital energy; the compositions are more studied, yet not mannered; the typically Michelangelo habit of contrasts is not limited to apparently painful contortions in the individual figures, but includes entire scenes vibrating in unison. Although the use of color is restrained – in keeping with the chiaroscuro technique – its choice contributed enormously to the overall effect: he alternates disparate colors and contrasts the cold hard tones with opaque ones. It is in this part of the chapel that Michelangelo's pictorial language reaches maturity and becomes the only legitimate alternative to Raphael's eclectic classicism as well as the basic text for the dominant school of painters in 16th century Italy.

Not as obvious, but nonetheles of great historical importance in Michelangelo's evolution as an artist, is his work on the « Ancestors of Christ » in the lunettes. Here, the extensive use of contrasts (the « contrapposto ») for expressionistic purposes, and of the harsh – invariably monochromatic – tones, create a feeling of cold torment. This prepares the dramatic spiritual mood of early Roman mannerism.

THE TAPESTRIES

The tapestries were an integral part of the decorations in the Sistine Chapel. Commissioned by Pope Leo X, Raphael drew the cartoon designs between 1515 and 1516 and sent them on to Brussels where they were woven with *Scenes of the Lives of St. Peter and St. Paul*. The whole series was completed by 1524 and hung that year immediately below the 15th century frescoes. After the Sack of Rome, the tapestries were scattered around a number of times. They are now on exhibit in the Vatican Museums. Raphael's cartoons had another fate. After having been woven into tapestries several times in Brussels (results today in Berlin, Dresden, Madrid, Urbino, Loreto, and Mantua), they were finally purchased by Charles I of England on the advice of the painter Rubens. Today, they are on exhibit in the Victoria and Albert Museum in London.

Aside from their extraordinary artistic value, the tapestries had a specific pictorial significance in keeping with the themes of the chapel: the work and miracles of Peter, the first Pope, and of the first evangelizer, Paul, mark the historical moment of the transfer of the gospel message from Jerusalem to Rome. They represent the justification for the spiritual primacy of the Pontifical See as the center of Christianity. The tapestries therefore were a purposeful link between the frescoes – that speak of the coming redemption – and of the Last Judgment – where the drama of a sinning and redeemed mankind is concluded.

THE LAST JUDGMENT

Twenty years after the completion of the ceiling, Michelangelo returned to work again in the Sistine Chapel. Paul III Farnese nurtured an idea – perhaps vividly recalling the Sack of Rome – of his predecessor Clement VII. The *Last Judgment* was planned for the present altar wall (in a conspicuous place, indeed, just as pictorial tradition would dictate) as a perennial warning about the frailty of life and the universe. After lengthy negotiations, Michelangelo set to work in May, 1536 (or perhaps even as early as the summer of 1535). The official inauguration took place on Christmas, 1541.

The focal point of the immense composition is Christ's gesture of malediction. He appears high up the center of the wall, an open expanse beneath him. Under the biblically awesome power of his gesture, a whirlpool seems to rise and engulf the entire celestial scene – saints and virgins, prophets, martyrs, apostles. We can identify St. John the Baptist (in camel skin), St. Peter (with keys), St.

Andrew (with a cross), St. Lawrence (with grill), St. Bartholomew (with his own limp flesh on which the artist painted an anguished self-portrait), St. Simon (with saw), St. Blaise (with the wool-carder's comb), St. Catherine (with wheel), St. Sebastian (with arrows). The whirlpool spares only the Virgin Mary, drawn into her own sorrow, and then extends upwards to encompass scenes in the lunettes – the « Exaltation of the Cross » and « The Instruments of the Passion. »

Once again Christ's gesture is the gravitational force of a second vortex that moves violently up and down creating a heaving sea in which angels and the damned, demons and the resurrected, appear to bob. Caught in the movement are the elect – who rise to heaven along the left side – and the damned – falling down along the left side while vainly fighting the avenging angels. In the center, the wide open expanse is reserved for the shrill of the last judgment trumpet. The open expanse serves then as a sounding board over which the excited agitation of the individual groups increases until it reaches the highest level of tolerance. Below, out of the whirlpool, are two separate scenes. On the left is the resurrection of the dead, painfully and tortuously returning to life. Charon and his boat, on the right, epitomize in the oarsman's violent gesture and in the anonymous accumulation of cadavers, all the despair of hell.

The sources and meaning of Michelangelo's masterpiece have been the subject of polemical conjectures almost as soon as the fresco was unveiled. Vasari saw in it the culmination of all Italian pictorial art; citing some of its sources, he mentions Dante and Signorelli. Pietro Aretino, on the other hand, malevolently criticized it, finding hints of heresy in it and denouncing the scandal of so many nudes in a sacred place. Unfortunately, his criticism found its mark: Daniele da Volterra, a favorite Michelangelo pupil, was deputed to « put breeches » on the nudes. What was the original like? We can reconstruct it by comparing copies, such as those (now in Naples) which Marcello Venusti sketched immediately before the solemn unveiling. The accusations and exaggerations, redolent of the counter-reformation spirit, explain some of the polemics the work aroused. But Michelangelo's was a tough, well-tried faith, a spirituality tested and lived in the context of the Renaissance but with profound roots in the middle ages. The pictorial inspiration is clearly from the Italian « Quattrocento » (Giotto, Camposanto di Pisa, Orcagna). In fact, Michelangelo emphasized the ideal aspect by uniting time and space in a single vision and traditional divisions into sections. The drama before the viewer is unique and instantaneous and is acted out beyond time and space in the human sense.

Through this painting, Michelangelo relives – in spirit – the texts that modern experts point to as his possible sources: the Sacred Scriptures, the Divine Comedy, the Dies Irae hymn, and even the sermons of Savonarola. Just as for the ceiling, searching for the one single specific source inspiring the Last Judgment would be an abortive effort. We should rather speak of hints, of suggestions, which at times may even be quotations (for example, the figures of Charon, of Minos, of the devils shouldering the damned – all obviously inspired by Dante). In general, however, all the hints and suggestions were useful only in feeding the artist's meditation on the theme of death and judgment. Precisely because he did not adhere to a preconceived, rigid, pattern, but rather to a mental concept, Michelangelo could adopt the unusual, even heterodox, solutions that disconcerted his contemporaries: angels without wings; saints without haloes; horned and gruesome demons with grotesque grimaces. The images he conjures up are each a synthesis, almost ascetically pure, that has no significance of its own but only as part of that huge universal drama. Renaissance style is altered in order to express totally new subjects, an anguished reactionary spirituality, a warning as eloquent as Savonarola's on the vanity of things and on the implacable finality of the last judgment.

Conclusion

In summary, the pictorial decoration of the Sistine Chapel covers four distinct periods extending across more than half a century. Nevertheless, there is an extraordinary continuity in concept and merits to be called « a plan designed by Providence. » Overall, the various elements unite into one great cycle describing the history of mankind – from creation to sin, to redemption, to the end of the world. This unity, however, should not blind us to the fact that each element is anchored in a specific moment of history and for an historically defined purpose; and that, therefore, it reflects a particular moment of Italian Renaissance culture.

The frescoes represent the Reign of Law and the Reign of Grace which Christ continued through his vicars. In terms of 15th century spirituality, this is the culmination of the history of mankind. In spite of the presence of so many artists in the Sistine Chapel – all in the Florentine humanistic tradition – the pictorial plans, the hagiographic content, and the didactic purpose are all derived from the paleochristian basilicas. This means that the culture of the papal court did not yet include salient features of the already widespread Italian Renaissance.

On the ceiling, Michelangelo's magnificent Creation, Sin, and Expectation logically precede the cycles on the walls; but the spirit in which these were created is totally different. Michelangelo saw creation and sin as dramas of all mankind, and the Redemption as an act of faith and hope achieved always and everywhere. Through the spectacles of his neo-platonism, Michelangelo saw man unlike the one in catechisms or in the Sacred Scriptures; he saw a deeply profound spirituality. Along with the commemorative and hagiographic content of the paintings on the walls is the free profession of faith.

Raphael's series of tapestries, on the other hand, stressed the historical, not straying far from his own tomes. This was because the papal court wished to emphasize the source and validity of the Pope's powers as successor and vicar of Christ. The continuity of the series on the wall – ending with the pontiffs – was done in an entirely different spiritual climate. The objective was to confirm papal authority at a time when Protestant Reformers made it their principal target of criticism against the Catholic Church. It is not by chance that this « historical » spirit prevailed in the Rome of Leo X, a Rome that claimed to be – and perhaps was – the moral and political capital of Renaissance civilization.

The last fresco painted in the Sistine Chapel, the *Last Judgment*, depicts not only the conclusion of all human vicissitudes – the moment when all who hoped for the coming of the Messiah or accepted his gospel, or contributed to his triumph through his Church, find themselves together before Christ the Judge – but also, thanks to the tormented yet strong faith Michelangelo poured into it, an abiding warning to all mankind in the face of death. It is here that we find the ultimate expression of the Italian Renaissance; the bitter condemnation of the dream of universal beauty, where vanity is finally, and in fact, understood.

Exterior view of the SISTINE CHAPEL before
Sixtus IV Della Rovere ordered Giovannino de' Dolci
(or Baccio Pontelli) to carry out the works of transformation.

INTERIOR of the SISTINE CHAPEL with the starred vault,
by Pier Matteo d'Amelia, before Michelangelo put his hand to it.
In the background can be seen the paintings and the two windows
that were removed to make place for the Last Judgment.

VATICAN – FULL VIEW of the SISTINE CHAPEL with
Michelangelo's CEILING and LAST JUDGMENT and also
the 15TH CENTURY FRESCOES on the lateral walls. ▶

THE UPPER AREA:

1. MICHELANGELO: Lunette of the Ancestors of Christ – *Prince Nahshon on the right and his future wife on the left.*

2. MICHELANGELO: Lunette of the Ancestors of Christ – *with the aged David and Solomon on the left and Bathsheba on the right.*

3. MICHELANGELO: Lunette of the Ancestors – *Jehoshaphat on the left and young Joram embracing his mother on the right.*

4. MICHELANGELO: Lunette of the Ancestors – *Meshullemeth rocking Amon on the left and the repentant Manasseh on the right.*

5. MICHELANGELO: Lunette of the Ancestors – *Josiah and the little Jeconiah on the right, Shealtiel with his mother on the left.*

6. MICHELANGELO: Lunette of the Ancestors – *Azor and young Zadok on the left and a « philosopher » on the right.*

7. MICHELANGELO: Lunette of the Ancestors – *Prince Amminadab on the left, a woman combing her hair on the right.*

8. MICHELANGELO: Lunette of the Ancestors – *King Boaz on the right and his wife Ruth with Obed on the left.*

9. MICHELANGELO: Lunette of the Ancestors – *the child Abijah with a woman on the left, a sleeping figure on the right.*

10. MICHELANGELO: Lunette of the Ancestors – *Jotham and his son Ahaz on the left and a woman on the right.*

11. MICHELANGELO: Lunette of the Ancestors – *Zerubbabel and Abiud on the right, Eliakim and his mother on the left.*

12. MICHELANGELO: Lunette of the Ancestors – *Achim and Eliud on the left, the mother of Eliud nursing a son on the right.*

ON THE INTERMEDIATE ZONE, a series of 24 POPES:

1. St. Anacletus, Greek (76-88) and St. Alexander I, Roman (105-115).

2. St. Telesphorus, Greek (126-136) and St. Pius I of Aquileia (140-155).

3. St. Soter of Fondi (166-175) and St. Victor I, African (189-199).

4. St. Callistus I, Roman (217-222) and St. Pontian, Roman (230-235).

5. St. Fabian, Roman (236-250) and St. Lucius I, Roman (253-254).

6. St. Sixtus II, Greek (257-258) and St. Felix I, Roman (269-274).

7. St. Clement, Roman (88-97) and St. Evaristus, Greek (97-105).

8. St. Sixtus I, Roman (115-125) and St. Hyginus, Greek (136-140).

9. St. Anicetus, Syrian (155-166) and St. Eleutherius of Epirus (175-189).

10. St. Zephyrinus, Roman (199-217) and St. Urban I, Roman (222-230).

11. St. Anterus, Greek (235-236) and St. Cornelius, Roman (151-153).

12. St. Stephen, Roman (254-257) and St. Dionysius, Roman (259-268).

THE LOWER AREA, THE FIFTEENTH CENTURY FRESCOES:

1. P. PERUGINO: THE BAPTISM OF CHRIST IN THE JORDAN, *in the center: St. John the Baptist preaching and a sermon by Christ.*

2. S. BOTTICELLI: THE TEMPTATIONS OF CHRIST *illustrated in the background; in the foreground: the purification of the leper according to the rite prescribed by Moses.*

3. D. GHIRLANDAIO: THE CALL OF ST. PETER AND ST. ANDREW. *In the background, Christ calls the two brothers and two other Apostles.*

4. C. ROSSELLI: THE SERMON ON THE MOUNT. *On the right: Christ heals a leper.*

5. P. PERUGINO: JESUS HANDING THE KEYS TO ST. PETER. *In the background: the episode of the tax money and also the attempt to stone Christ.*

6. C. ROSSELLI: THE LAST SUPPER. *Seen through the windows in the background: the prayer in the Garden of Gethsemane, the kiss of Judas, and the Crucifixion.*

7. P. PERUGINO: MOSES' JOURNEY INTO EGYPT. *Moses takes leave of Jethro (background); Moses stopped by an angel (foreground). On the right, Zipporah circumcizes the son of Moses.*

8. S. BOTTICELLI: MOSES RECEIVES THE CALL. *After his escape from the Pharaoh, Moses defends the daughters of Jethro. While tending the flock on Mount Horeb, he hears the divine command and leaves for Egypt with his whole family.*

9. C. ROSSELLI: THE CROSSING OF THE RED SEA. *The Hebrews are safe on the shore, while the waters engulf the Egyptian army.*

10. C. ROSSELLI: ADORATION OF THE GOLDEN BULL. *On Mount Sinai, God gives the tablets of the commandments to Moses (upper part). After his descent from the mountain, Moses presents the tablets to the people. Scorned, he breaks the tablets and punishes all who adored the golden bull (upper part, right).*

11. S. BOTTICELLI: THE PUNISHMENT OF KORAH, DATHAN, AND ABIRAM *who, with their followers, rebelled against Moses (on the right). Moses challenges them; when they fail, the rebels are swallowed up by the earth.*

12. L. SIGNORELLI: THE LAST DAYS OF MOSES. *The law-giver proclaims the Law; after having seen the Promised Land from Mount Nebo, Moses comes down and entrusts the staff to Joshua. In the background, on the left, the death of Moses.*

Sistine Chapel – P. PERUGINO:

MOSES' JOURNEY INTO EGYPT.

*This fresco carries the title: « The observance of the old regeneration
through the circumcision of Moses. » We see an illustration of
a passage from Exodus (Chap. IV, 18-20): After receiving the
command from Yahweh, Moses takes leave of his father-in-law
Jethro (A) and with his wife Zipporah, his sons Gershom and Eliezer,
and entire household, takes off for Egypt. On the journey,
the Angel « came to meet him ... and tried to kill him » (Ex. IV, 24) (B).
Zipporah circumcizes Eliezer (C) while Moses and Gershom –
his first-born – observe the rite (D). The covenant with Yahweh is
strengthened and the mission of Moses is thus blessed.
The identity of the other figures is uncertain; some, however,
have recognized the features of Pinturicchio in the youth standing
immediately in back of Moses at the moment the latter
is confronted by the angel.*

Sistine Chapel – P. Perugino:
MOSES' JOURNEY INTO EGYPT.　31

Sistine Chapel – S. Botticelli:

MOSES RECEIVES THE CALL FROM GOD.

High on the fresco is the title: « The trials of Moses, promulgator of the written Law. » We find episodes from the Book of Exodus (Chap. II, III, IV): Moses slays the Egyptian who mistreats the Hebrew (A), the Hebrew helped by a woman (B). Moses escapes to Midian (C) where he puts to flight the shepherds who prevent the daughters of Jethro from watering their flock (D) and helps the girls (E). While shepherding his father-in-law's flock on Mount Horeb, he hears the call of Yahweh. Removing his shoes, he approaches the burning bush (F) and receives the command to return to Egypt to free the Hebrews from bondage (G). Armed with the staff of Yahweh, he leaves for Egypt with his wife Zipporah and his whole household (H).

Sistine Chapel – P. Perugino: MOSES' JOURNEY INTO EGYPT.
Detail: *Zipporah with her sons Gershom and Eliezer.*

Sistine Chapel – S. BOTTICELLI:
MOSES RECEIVES THE
CALL FROM GOD.

Sistine Chapel – S. BOTTICELLI:

THE PUNISHMENT OF KORAH, DATHAN, AND ABIRAM.

With their followers, they rebelled against the authority of Moses (A), refuse to acknowledge it and insist that Aaron is a usurper of the office of priest. They are put to the test.
The title reads: « The rebellion against Moses, the Law-giver. »
The Prophet, standing before the altar, invokes the name of Yahweh against the rebels (B), while their thurifers fall to the ground (C). Aaron alone is spared by God (D). The rebels, cursed by God, are swallowed by the earth (E) (Numbers, XVI, 1 sq), and their 250 followers are devoured by fire (id. vv. 31-35). The building at the right (F) has been identified as the « Settizonio », still standing (at the foot of the south side of the Palatine) during the reign of Sixtus IV. On the Arch of Titus, in the center (G), we read the inscription: « No one may claim the honor (of high priesthood) unless called by God as Aaron was. »
The second figure at the extreme right is perhaps Botticelli.

Sistine Chapel – S. BOTTICELLI: MOSES RECEIVES THE CALL FROM GOD. Detail: *Moses helps the daughters of Jethro.*

Sistine Chapel – S. Botticelli:
THE PUNISHMENT OF KORAH,
DATHAN, AND ABIRAM.   39

Sistine Chapel – L. Signorelli:

THE LAST DAYS OF MOSES.

The title on the painting reads: « Moses explaining the written Law. »
Nearing his end, the Prophet sits on a throne (A), with the book
of the Law which he explains and recommends to the attentive
people (B). At his feet, the Tablets of Mount Sinai
and a bowl with manna (C). In the center is a young nude (D)
very likely representing the tribe of Levi which was excluded from
the division of the Promised Land: the tribe of Levi would depend
exclusively upon the offerings received from religious cult.
High on the fresco, Moses perceives the Promised Land
from Mount Nebo (E) but he will never set foot there.
He descends from the mountain (F), entrusts the leader's staff
to Joshua (G) and dies (H) at Moab at the age of 120.

Sistine Chapel – S. Botticelli: THE PUNISHMENT
OF KORAH, DATHAN, AND ABIRAM. Detail: *Moses, Aaron, and the rebels.*

CRIPTAE · AMOIS

Sistine Chapel – L. Signorelli:
THE LAST DAYS OF MOSES.   43

Sistine Chapel – P. PERUGINO:

THE BAPTISM OF CHRIST IN THE JORDAN.

High on the fresco we see the (recently discovered) original title and name of the author: « The Establishment of the new regeneration through the Baptism of Christ. » « Done by Pietro Perugino from the City of Pieve. » High on the painting, God the Father (A). In the foreground, the Baptism of Christ (B) with dove above his head (Mt III, 13 sq). In the background: the sermon of the Precursur (C), John the Baptist approaches the River Jordan (D) and Christ preaching (E). The identity of the other figures in the central area is uncertain.

Sistine Chapel – L. SIGNORELLI: THE LAST DAYS OF MOSES.
Detail: *Moses entrusts the leader's staff to Joshua.*

OPVS·PETRI·PERVSINI·CASTRO·PLEBIS

OPVS·PETRI·PERVSINI·CASTRO·PLEBIS

Sistine Chapel – P. Perugino:
THE BAPTISM OF CHRIST
IN THE JORDAN.

47

Sistine Chapel – S. Botticelli:

THE TEMPTATIONS OF CHRIST.

The title reads: « The temptations of Christ, the legislator of the Gospel. » Satan, disguised as a Franciscan friar, tempts Jesus who is weak after his long fast in the desert (A); he carries Christ to the pinnacle of the Temple and tempts him again (B); defeated for the third time on a high mountain, the demons throws away the robe and disappears. Angels draw near and serve food to Christ (Mt IV) (C). After Christ descends from the mountain, he observes the ritual purification of the leper (D) whom he had just healed (Mk 1, 40). The complex rite takes place in the foreground (E) according to Leviticus XIV, 1 sq.
The central building represents the Santo Spirito Hospital in Rome, founded by Sixtus IV Della Rovere whose family crest is alluded to by the two oak trees. The two figures at the extreme right are probably Botticelli and Filippino Lippi.

Sistine Chapel – P. Perugino: THE BAPTISM OF CHRIST
IN THE JORDAN. Detail: *Christ and John the Baptist.*

Sistine Chapel – S. Botticelli:
THE TEMPTATIONS OF CHRIST. 51

Sistine Chapel – S. Botticelli: THE TEMPTATIONS OF CHRIST. Detail: *Christ, Satan and the Angels.*

Sistine Chapel – C. Rosselli:

THE LAST SUPPER.

The title above the fresco reads:
« Repetition of the Gospel Law by Christ. »
In the foreground, we see the Savior in the midst of His disciples
blessing and breaking bread (Mt. XXVI, 26).
Facing Him is Judas ready to leave for the betrayal. Unlike the
other disciples Judas has an opaque halo and on his shoulder
sit the demon tempter (Lk. XXII, 3).
Through the three windows we see: The Prayer in the Garden,
The Kiss of Judas and The Crucifixion.
The four figures on the sides have not been identified.

53

Sistine Chapel – C. Rosselli:
THE LAST SUPPER.

Sistine Chapel – P. PERUGINO: JESUS HANDING THE KEYS TO ST. PETER.
Detail: *Christ confers upon Peter the power of the Keys.*

Sistine Chapel – P. PERUGINO:

JESUS HANDING THE KEYS TO ST. PETER.

The painting is titled: « The rebellion against Jesus Christ, the legislator. » Jesus, in the foreground, confers upon Peter the power of the keys (Mt XVI, 19) (A).
In back, on the vast multi-colored marble pavement, we see two episodes from the Gospels: the Pharisees seeking to compromise Christ about tax money (Mt XXII, 17 sq) (B) and the attempted stoning of Christ (John VIII, 59 – X, 31 sq) (C).
In the background, the Temple of Jerusalem dominates the scene (D).
It is in Renaissance style, flanked by two arches similar to those of the Arch of Constantine (E) which bears an inscription praising Sixtus IV for emulating Solomon in building the Sistine Chapel, and announcing him superior to Solomon, if not in wealth, at least in piety.
Among the spectators at the scene, the following have been identified: Alfonso di Calabria (1), Perugino himself (2), Pinturicchio (3), the assistant Bartolomeo della Gatta (some say Baccio Pontelli) (4), and Giovannino de' Dolci (5), the architect of the Sistine Chapel.

Sistine Chapel – P. Perugino:
JESUS HANDING THE
KEYS TO ST. PETER.

59

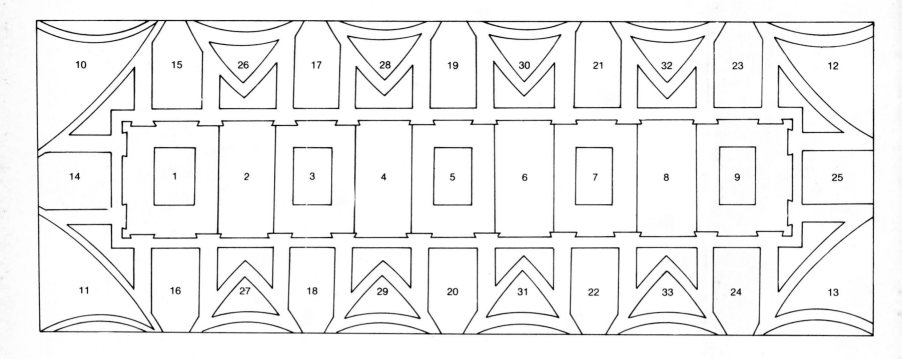

THE SISTINE CHAPEL'S VAULT

1. God Dividing Light from Darkness.
2. Creation of the Sun and the Moon.
3. God Separating Waters from the Land.
4. The Creation of Man.
5. The Creation of Woman.
6. The Original Sin.
7. The Sacrifice of Noah.
8. The Deluge.
9. The Drunkenness of Noah.
10. The Punishment of Haman.
11. The Brazen Serpent.
12. David and Goliath.
13. Judith and Holophernes.
14. The Prophet Jonah.
15. The Prophet Jeremiah.
16. The Lybian Sibyl.
17. The Persian Sibyl.
18. The Prophet Daniel.
19. The Prophet Ezekiel.
20. The Cumaean Sibyl.
21. The Erythrean Sibyl.
22. The Prophet Isaiah.
23. The Prophet Joel.
24. The Delphic Sibyl.
25. The Prophet Zechariah.
26. The child Solomon with his moter.
27. The Parents of future King Jesse.
28. The child Rehoboam with his mother. In the background, Solomon.
29. The child Asa with his father, and sleeping mother.
30. The child Josiah with his mother and father Joram, and one of his brothers.
31. The child Hezekiah with his mother, and father Ahaz.
32. The child Zerubbabel with his mother, and his father Shealtiel.
33. The child Josiah with his mother, and his father Amon.

The first VIEW of the complete VAULT OF THE SISTINE CHAPEL was made in 1961 after a long study. With the aid of more modern technical means and at high cost, curvatures of the Vault were concealed and an image without deformation of perspective was obtained.

Ceiling of the Sistine
Chapel – MICHELANGELO:
THE SEPARATION OF
LIGHT FROM
DARKNESS (GEN. I, 4).
*At either side, a twin pair
of Nudes holding up two
gilded bronze medallions.
The left medallion shows
the sacrifice of Abraham
(GEN. XXII, 9); the one
on the right depicts
Elijah carried up to
heaven in a fiery chariot
(II KGS, II, 11).*

71

Ceiling of the Sistine Chapel –
MICHELANGELO:
THE CREATION OF THE
SUN AND MOON AND
THE PLANTS (GEN. I, 11, 16).

72   *The Creator appears twice.*

Ceiling of the Sistine
Chapel – MICHELANGELO:
DIVIDING THE
WATERS FROM
THE LAND
(GEN. I, 9). *Of the two
gilded bronze medallions,
the first has no pictorial
representation; the second
depicts the Death of Absalom*
(II SAMUEL, XVIII, 9 sq.)   75

Ceiling of the
Sistine Chapel –
MICHELANGELO:
THE DELPHIC
SIBYL, *much admired
for her extraordinary
beauty. In the center,
two Genii.*

Ceiling of the Sistine Chapel – MICHELANGELO: THE SACRIFICE OF NOAH.
The patriarch leaves the ark after the deluge with his wife, his sons and their wives.
He builds an altar and offers up animals in sacrifice of thanksgiving to God (GEN. VIII, 20).

Ceiling of the Sistine Chapel – MICHELANGELO: THE DELUGE

This is the first biblical narrative Buonarroti painted on the ceiling

In the center, an overloaded barge is on the verge of sinking. In the
background, the shipwreched trying to grasp hold of the Ark of Noah (GEN. VII).

Ceiling of the Sistine
Chapel – MICHELANGELO:
THE DRUNKENNESS
OF NOAH. *The drunken
Noah sleeps in the nude
in the presence of his sons.
Shem and Japheth cover his
nakedness, but Ham, in the
foreground, jeers him
derisively* (GEN. IX, 20 sq).

89

IONAS

Ceiling of the Sistine Chapel – MICHELANGELO: THE PROPHET JONAH. *The figure of the Prophet stands above the Last Judgment. On the right, the whale that swallowed him and released him three days later. The episode allegorically prefigures the burial and resurrection of Christ* (MT. XII, 40).

Ceiling of the
Sistine Chapel –
MICHELANGELO:
Detail of the
ERITREAN SIBYL.

A – CELESTIAL WORLD

1 - *Christ the Judge*
2 - *The Madonna*
3 - *St. Lawrence*
4 - St. Martha, or St. Anne
5 - St. Andrew
6 - Rachel, or Dante's Beatrice
7 - Noah, or Enoch, or Paul III
8 - St. John the Baptist, or Adam
9 - Abraham, or St. Bernard, or Pope Julius II
10 - Abel
11-12 - Niobe and a daughter, or Eve and a daughter, or Maternity personified, or the Church Merciful and a believer
13 - The daughter of Pharaoh who found Moses, or Sarah, or Eve
14 - The Archangel Gabriel carrying the Cross
14a - An Archangel carrying the Column
15 - Francesco Amadori, Duke of Urbino, or Tommaso de' Cavalieri
16 - *St. Bartholomew* (with features of P. Aretino)
17 - *St. Bartholomew's flesh resembling Michelangelo*
18 - St. Mark (Pope Clement VII)
19 - *St. Paul*
20 - *St. Peter*
21 - Job, or Adam, or Abraham
22 - Job's wife, or Eve
23 - St. Longinus
24 - St. Simon Zealot
25 - St. Philip, or the Penitent Thief
26 - *St. Catherine of Alexandria*
27 - *St. Blaise*
28 - *St. Sebastian*
29 - The Penitent Thief, or St. Francis of Assisi, or St. Andrew, or St. Simon of Cyrene, or Justice personified, or Symbol of Man and his pains
30 - Moses, or Adam
31 - Dante Alighieri

B – ANGELIC TRUMPETERS

32 - The Archangel Michael with the Book of the Elect

C – RESURRECTION OF THE DEAD

33 - Dante
34 - Michelangelo, or Pope Julius II, a helpful monk, or Martin Luther
35 - Michelangelo
36 - Savonarola

D – BLESSED SOULS ASCENDING TO HEAVEN

37-38-39 - A Blessed One (or an Angel raising two blacks)

E – THE DAMNED DRAGGED INTO HELL AND THE NETHER REGION

40 - A prideful man, or one damned for losing hope (in contraposition to Christian Hope)
41 - A demon
42 - A prideful man, or a sluggard
43 - A miser, or the simoniac Pope Nicholas III
44 - A wrathful man, or a prideful man
45 - A lustful man
46-47 - Paolo and Francesca da Rimini
48 - A prideful man, or a cheat
49 - *Charon*, or Satan with the features of the Constable of Bourbon
50 - Caesar Borgia
51 - Minos with the features of Biagio da Cesena
52 - Count Ugolino of Pisa, and Archbishop Ruggieri

Sistine Chapel –
Michelangelo: Full view of
THE LAST JUDGMENT.

A Copy of THE LAST JUDGMENT, executed in 1549 by
Marcello Venusti, pupil of Michelangelo, for Cardinal Alessandro.
The painting, measuring 1,90 × 1,45 meters, is currently preserved
in the Museo di Capodimonte, Naples. It is an important document
indispensable for a comparative study of the original
(unretouched by Daniele da Volterra)
and the present condition of the masterpiece.

Sistine Chapel – MICHELANGELO: THE LAST JUDGMENT.
Detail *of angels heralding the judgment with their trumpets
and carrying the books of good works and evil works.*

Sistine Chapel – MICHELANGELO: THE LAST JUDGMENT.
Detail *of Christ the Judge and the Virgin Mary.* ▶

Sistine Chapel – MICHELANGELO: THE LAST JUDGMENT.
Detail *of the demon Charon ferrying the souls to hell. Awaiting*

them at the extreme right is Minos with his serpentine tail and ears of an ass (caricature of Biagio da Cesena who criticized Michelangelo).

Sistine Chapel –
MICHELANGELO:
THE LAST JUDGMENT.
Detail: *One of the damned
dragged to hell by demons.*

Sistine Chapel –
MICHELANGELO:
THE LAST JUDGMENT.
Detail: *To the right of the
Virgin Mary, St. John
the Baptist (Adam?) waiting
in a group of the Blessed for
the verdict of judgment.*

Sistine Chapel – Michelangelo: THE LAST JUDGMENT.
Detail: *At the right of Christ, in a group of Blessed,*
St. Bartholomew displays the knife and flesh of his martyrdom.
Michelangelo's self-portrait appears in the folds of the flesh.

THE RAPHAEL STANZAS

Raphael Sanzio was only twenty-five when he left Florence for Rome in 1508 to paint the frescoes in the new apartments the Holy Father chose to occupy. The commission was given by Julius II Della Rovere who no longer cared to stay in the rooms once occupied by his predecessor, Alexander VI Borgia. He took instead a four room apartment on the top floor. Three of the four rooms were of modest dimensions and had once served as part of the residence of Pope Nicholas V. The fourth was considerably larger and dated back to the 13th century Pope, Nicholas III. With the completion of the work, these rooms were forever afterwards called « The Raphael Stanzas. » They comprise the *Stanza of the Borgo Fire*, the *Stanza of the Signature*, the *Stanza of Heliodorus*, and the *Stanza of Constantine*.

At the turn of the 15th century, several artists collaborated in decorating the rooms. They were Piero della Francesca, Bramantino, Frà Bartolomeo della Gatta, and Luca Signorelli. Julius II also called upon Sodoma, Lorenzo Lotto, and Perugino to complete the work. But when Raphael arrived in Rome at the end of 1508, the Pope ordered the works destroyed. This signalled the beginning of the richest and greatest series of Renaissance paintings from the stand-point both of doctrinal content and stylistic development.

I. The Stanza of the Signature (1508-1511)

No doubt it was a scholar of the papal court – someone of the stature of Calcagnini, Ariosto, or Inghirami – who, with papal approval, planned the decorative theme for the first room Raphael was to fresco. The decision was taken – the great neo-platonic concepts of Truth, Good, and Beauty would be glorified in painting. This distinctively humanist theme was probably selected in view of the eventual use destined for the room: it was to serve as the Pope's library, or so Paolo Giovio, writing at the time, informs us.

The room became known as the *Stanza of the Signature* because as soon as the work was completed, the most important papal documents were signed and sealed here. The frescoed walls represent the major masterpieces personally painted by the young master from Urbino – The *Dispute on the Blessed Sacrament* and the *School of Athens* – exalting revealed Truth and natural Truth. The concept of Beauty, inspired by poetry, is depicted in the *Mount Parnassus* fresco. Good is pictorially represented in the *Theological and Cardinal Virtues* and in *Law*, both ecclesiastical (*St. Raymond of Peñafort Presenting the Decretals to Gregory IX*) and civil (*The Emperor Justinian Handing the Pandects to Trebonianus*). The decoration of the ceiling re-echoes the same concepts by personifying them.

Raphael rejected abstractions, symbols, and allegories in pictorially interpreting the universal concepts of Truth, Beauty, and Good; instead, his creative and innovative genius, seized upon « illustrious personalities » who, in the flesh, give movement, light, color, and life to the philosophical content of these abstract concepts.

« Triumph of the Church and of the Faith » would be a more suitable title for the scene of the *Dispute on the Blessed Sacrament*. In this fresco, in fact, Raphael shows us God, the Supreme Truth, contemplated in beatific vision in heaven and adored in faith on earth under the appearance of the consecrated Host. The focal point, the core of the pictorial composition where all the lines of vision converge, is the Eucharistic Bread. The Eucharist – Heaven's own loving gift to the world and at the same time an invitation to join the Holy Trinity – is on an axis that joins the Host to the Trinity. Around this central axis, deployed in a double layer of semicircles, the whole Church militant and triumphant gathers in contemplation.

At the top of the lunette, the Eternal Father appears in the act of blessing between two choirs of angels. Immediately below, surrounded by a great aureola, is his Incarnate Son, the adoring Madonna in an attitude of prayer, and St. John the Baptist. Below these figures is the Holy Spirit, the Inspirer of the four Gospels pictured as open books. Seated on clouds on either side of the central group are the Blessed of the Old and the New Testament – the Church triumphant. We see, from the left, St. Peter, Adam, St. John the Evangelist, David, St. Lawrence, and a prophet; on the right, Judas Maccabee (?), St. Stephen, Moses, St. James Lesser, Abraham, and St. Paul. Each is recognized by some characteristic detail.

In the lower band of the fresco we see the Fathers of the Church and several theologians – the Church militant – discussing the mystery of the Eucharist. Thanks to Vasari who provided a lengthy (although not always accurate) description of the Stanzas, we can identify the personalities in this group. « There are, » writes Vasari, « Francis, Thomas Aquinas, Bonaventure, Scotus, Niccolò de Lira, Dante (considered a theologian by his contemporaries), Frà Girolamo Savonarola da Ferrara, and all the Christian theologians plus an infinity of portraits. » The last observation is interesting; in fact, on the far left, the aged Dominican with eyes raised to heaven is probably Frà Angelico; St. Gregory, intently contemplating the Host, has the features of Julius II; on the right, we easily recognize the dignified, solemn figure of Sixtus IV, the uncle of Julius II; behind Sixtus is the laurel-crowned Dante; and finally, Savonarola almost entirely covered by his black hood.

The carefully planned and balanced composition suggests the strong influence of Perugino; but it already enjoys that harmony which Raphael went on to perfect in his next work, the *School of Athens*.

This fresco represents natural Truth. Under the vault of an immense basilica (inspired by Constantine's in the Roman Forum), decorated with statues of Apollo and Minerva, a crowd of philosophers and wise men of the past argue heatedly among themselves or meditate in silence. In the center we see Plato (long white beard and the features of Leonardo da Vinci), text of the *Timaeus* in hand, the other hand pointing to heaven, the « seat of the ideas. » At his side is Aristotle, in turn holding his *Ethics* and pointing to the earth. The two philosophers and their graphic gesturing make a point which is the core of the philosophy of Marsilio Ficino: Aristotle's gesture symbolizes the positive spirit; the vertical gesture of Plato alludes to a superior quality, the contemplation of ideas.

After Vasari, others have tried to identify the personalities in the central group, but there continues to be disagreement among scholars. On the left, cloaked in olive mantle, is Socrates (faunlike profile) arguing in a group that includes

Critias, Xenophon, and Alcibiades. Facing a venerable old man (Zeno?) is Epicurus, crowned with grape leaves, presumably defending hedonism. Attentively followed bu his pupils (among whom is the turbanned Averroes) Pythagoras teaches the diatesseron from a book. In strong contrast in front of him is Xenocrates (others say Parmenides). In the foreground, head resting on his arm, the mournfully meditating Heracleitus. The absence of this figure in the original cartoon (now in Milan's Ambrosian Museum) and the obvious Michelangelo style, lead one to believe that Raphael added this figure in 1511 when, after completing the room, he saw the first half of the Sistine Chapel ceiling. In tribute to his great rival, Raphael portrayed Michelangelo in the figure of the philosopher from Ephesus. The child at the side of Epicurus, clearly indifferent to the speculations of the philosophers, seems to be Federico Gonzaga. The passerby, in white translucent toga and da Vinci smile, is supposedly Francesco Maria Della Rovere. Further to the right, calmly stretched out on the stairs, is Diogenes, the object of the remonstrations by the disciples of the Academy. In the foreground, to the right of Aristotle, Raphael portrayed Bramante in the person of Euclid, bending over a table and demonstrating a theorem with the help of a compass. Bramante – the great architect of Julius II – was responsible for Raphael's call to Rome. Raphael chose the gold border of Euclid's (Bramante) tunic for his own signature: R.V.S.M., that is, « Raphael Urbinas Sua Manu » (by the hand of Raphael of Urbino). Further to the right, identified by the crown he wears, is the geographer Ptolemy (confused with the Egyptian dynasty of the same name) holding the globe of the earth. Facing him is the astronomer Zoroaster, holding the globe of the sky. The young man at their side and facing the viewer is supposedly Raphael himself in the company of Sodoma (white mantle), the artist who preceded Raphael in the decoration of the ceiling of this room.

The optical illusion in the *Dispute* and the *School of Athens* and the impression of vastness they suggest, are not as evident on the other two walls. There were surface problems. Raphael was obliged to take into consideration the door and the window. Nevertheless, he achieved exceptional results in this less than suitable space by extending the illusion of perspective and decentralizing the compositions.

The concept of Beauty is symbolically illustrated in the *Mount Parnassus* where we see Apollo playing his lyre (sweet tones) in the presence of the nine Muses (at Apollo's feet sit the beautiful Calliope – the Muse of epic poetry –with horn; and Terpsichore, the Muse of lyric poetry, who holds the zither) and of great poets ancient and contemporary. We see the blind Homer scanning the sky while Ennius writes down the verses he dictates, Behind them is Dante (in cameo profile) who answers Virgil. The figure at their side is probably Statius. In the foreground and to the left is the gracefully reclining figure of Sappho, in blue and white garment with gold adornments. She turns towards Alcaeus, Corinna, Petrarch (whose head can be seen peeking from behind a tree) and Anacreon. Identifying the figures on the opposite side is more difficult; the fifth from the end (white beard, profile) could be Tebaldeo facing Boccaccio, Tibullus, and Ariosto. In the foreground, finger to his lips, is Ovid; together with Sannazzaro, he converses with Horace.

On the opposite lunette, the *Cardinal and Theological Virtues* represent *subjective* Good. Strength holds an oak branch (crest of Julius II Della Rovere);

Prudence, shown with two faces, looks intently into a mirror; while Temperance holds the reins. Justice is portrayed on the ceiling of this room. Faith, Hope, and Charity – the theological virtues – are depicted as cherubs. Faith points heavenward; Hope holds a torch; and Charity shakes the acorns from the tree of Strength.

Below the window, *objective* Good, object of ecclesiastical and civil law, is illustrated by two historical scenes. To the left, *St. Raymond of Peñafort Presents the Decretals to Gregory IX* (another portrait of Julius II with three of his favorite cardinals – Giovanni de' Medici, later Pope Clement VII; behind him is Alexander Farnese, later Pope Paul III; and Antonio del Monte). On the right, *Emperor Justinian Hands the Pandects to Trebonianus*. These two frescoes are far below Raphael's usual standards; they were probably the work of the French artist, Guillaume de Marcillat.

The wall frescoes are Raphael's, but the ceiling was done by others. The decorative composition of the ceiling's central octagon – crests of the Church surrounded by winged cherubs – was there when Raphael began frescoing in 1508. He then planned the four basic ideas which his assistants reflected in the four subjects depicted on the walls. Above the *Dispute* is Theology; above the *Virtues*, Justice; above the *School of Athens*, Philosophy (flanked by the statues of Diana of Ephesus, the symbol of fertility); above the *Parnassus*, Poetry. The four rectangular scenes are also related to the same theme. Part of this work may be Sodoma's, namely *Adam and Eve* (prelude to the coming of Christ), the *Judgment of Solomon* (another aspect of objective Good), *Astronomy* (an allusion to science), and *Apollo and Marcia* (glorifying beauty).

II. The Stanza of Heliodorus (1511-1514)

Whereas the frescoes of the first Stanza express the noblest aspects of Renaissance classical thought and its efforts to unite with the spirituality of Christian thought, the pictorial plan for the *Stanza of Heliodorus* (decorated next in point of time) illustrates God's protection over his Church since the late middle ages. The forceful interventions of the warrior Pope, Julius II, were a decisive factor during this time. Little wonder then that we should see here scenes of the many important events during his reign.

With the change in perception, there is also a change – and increased maturity – in Raphael's style. Undisputed master of Tuscan design, the artist now concentrated on color. His genius for constant growth enables him to assimilate the skill of the Venetian masters such as Dosso, Lotto, and even his rival, Sebastiano del Piombo.

Here too the decoration of the ceiling was left to his disciples while Raphael began with the main scene *Heliodorus Pursued and Felled in the Temple*. We see Heliodorus after he breaks into the Temple with a confederate to steal of its treasures. Discovered by the faithful, he is pursued by them and by a horseman who joins them, and falls heavily to the ground. Meanwhile, oblivious to the excitement |around him, the priest Onias is deep in silent prayer near the altar. The allusion to enemies of the Church who infiltrated even the highest ranks is obvious and deliberate. But more! We find Julius II himself (carried on the pontifical chair) witnessing (and perhaps directing?) the apprehension of the bandit. At the Pope's side is the prelate G. Pietro dei Foliarii (the sketch is ambiguous; some believe this is a Raphael self-portrait); the two chair-bearers are traditionally identified as the engraver Marcantonio Raimondi, and Giulio Romano (here again some claim to recognize the features of Raphael). The whole fresco celebrates the finely honed skill of consummate composition: the violent diagonal movement rushing towards Heliodorus and then subtly repeated in the group clinging to the column; the open space in the center, revealing a deep perspective; on the opposite side, the rhythmic solemnity of the papal group and then the frightened women crouching alongside. Light accentuates the most dramatic segments of the action while the priest Onias has only the shadowy glimmer from the candelabra on the altar.

The *Mass at Bolsena* illustrates the miracle experienced by a priest from Bohemia who doubted the real presence of Christ in the Eucharist and then saw real blood issuing from the Sacred Host during his celebration of Mass at Bolsena. The miraculous event prompted Urban IV to institute the Feast of Corpus Christi which Sixtus IV revived. The fresco then is a tribute to the first Della Rovere Pope (Sixtus IV) and, at the same time, a commemoration of the successful Council of 1512. Again Raphael portrays Julius II (this time we find him to the right of the altar). Behind him are the aged Cardinal Riario and Cardinal Sangiorgio. As with *Parnassus*, Raphael found a difficult surface area to work on: it was broken with a window which itself was not even centered. He camouflaged this draw-back by designing the stairs asymmetrically. The result shows great strenght in composition and enhances the dynamism of its parts. With his range of colors, Raphael achieves extraordinary pure effects; one is led to think of some Venetian artist – a Lotto, for example – who at the time was in Rome. It is claimed that Lotto was responsible for the dark hues of the velvet worn by the Swiss Guards in the foreground.

The subject of the next fresco is the *Meeting of Leo I and Attila*. (The event took place near Mantua, not at the gates of Rome as Raphael's painting would lead us to believe). The historical encounter marked the end of the Hunnish invasion when St. Peter and St. Paul appeared to Attila. The calm, dignified figure of the Pope and his court contrasts sharply with the excited agitation of the bar-barians. Again, the Pope has the features of Julius II (an obvious allusion to the Battle of Ravenna in 1512). Behind the Pope stands Cardinal Medici, later to become Pope Leo X; further away is Paris de' Grassi. After the death of Julius II in March, 1513, his features were painted over in this scene and the likeness of the new Pope replaced it. Giovanni de' Medici therefore appears twice!

Raphael continued to give freer reign to his pupils, leaving to them the greater part of the execution. The lyric quality of the landscape in the distant horizon suggests the hand of Lorenzo Lotto.

In the last fresco of the *Stanza of Heliodorus*, Raphael again revolutionized his style and created the incomparable masterpiece, the *Liberation of St. Peter*. The setting was suggested by the titular church of Julius II, the Church of St. Peter in Chains. The painting is unlike anything in the history of art. Drawing inspiration from the *Acts of the Apostles*, the artist narrates how an angel frees St. Peter from his chains and leads him into the city while the guards are soundly asleep. Unusually striking is the contrasting intensity of the lights – from the illumination of the torch, from the moon, from the rays of breaking day, and from the almost phosforescent white of the angel. This mastery cannot be explained by a simple referral to the nightlight effects created by Pier della Francesca in the « Dream of Constantine » (preserved in Arezzo), as many scholars have done.

The paintings on the ceiling were done before Raphael. There is sufficient affinity of style between them and the two scenes relating to Justice in the *Stanza of the Signature* to attribute both to the hand of Guillaume de Marcillat. Just as in the *Stanza of the Signature*, the four episodes re-echo the large-scale scenes on the walls: the *Burning Bush* testifies to the power of God, invisible here as he was when Heliodorus was expelled from the Temple. *Jacob's Ladder* appears in a vision as did the angel to St. Peter. *God Appears to Noah*, allowing him to save the world, just as heavenly intervention put an end to the invasion of the Huns under Attila. Finally, the *Sacrifice of Abraham* is a witness to blind faith, to which the priest of the Bolsena Mass also gave proof.

III. The Stanza of the Borgo Fire (1514-1517)

The third Stanza worked on (the first in topographical order) further develops the political theme begun in the *Stanza of Heliodorus*. The events, however, have Leo X as the protagonist; he himself suggested the plan. The frescoes take events from the lives of two popes of the same name – Leo III and Leo IV – bearing the features of Leo X. The painting alludes to contemporary events. Raphael no longer has full direction of his pupils; they slowly free themselves from his influence and develop their own personal styles under the direction of Giulio Romano and Gianfrancesco Penni. Little wonder. Raphael was given other responsibilities in Rome at the time: in 1514 he took over from Bramante as chief architect of the new St. Peter's then being built; moreover, the following year he was named superintendent of antiquities. From this time he was perforce more concerned about architecture and antiquities than about the frescoes which he could only occasionally supervise and to wich he could rarely add his personal touch.

According to a passage in the *Liber Pontificalis*, the *Borgo Fire* occurred near the Vatican in 847 and was extinguished by the solemn blessing of Leo IV imparted from the Vatican Palace. The edifice depicted is the old Constantinian Basilica with the mosaic facade; it was razed early in the 16th century to make room for the new St. Peter's on which Raphael (after Bramante) was working. Roman monuments are clearly in evidence, but the setting is Troy. One of the most beautiful groupings illustrates a passage from Virgil: the hero Aeneas flees the city carrying his father Anchises on his shoulders while his little son, Ascanius, scurries alongside them. Together with the women in the foreground, this is without doubt, one of the Urbino Master's most impressive efforts. But the figures jumping from the wall betray a departure from classical harmony and a decline into « mannerism. » Giulio Romano contributed the imposing and dramatic figure of the woman carrying water.

The *Liber Pontificalis* also supplied information about the *Battle of Ostia* when, in 849, Leo IV and his army opposed the Saracen hordes. The fray, composed with consummate skill, is dominated by the imperious figure of Leo X. It is highly probable that Giulio Romano not only executed the painting, but was also the original designer of the work.

The other two scenes are notably weak. The first is the *Coronation of Charlemagne by Leo III* (probably a reference to the 1515 concordat signed by Leo X and Francis I) – a collaboration between the artists Penni and Raffaellino del Colle. The second represents the *Oath of Leo III*, who responded to the slanderous accusations of the nephews of Adrian I, reaffirming the principle that the Vicar of Christ is responsible to God alone. It is generally agreed that Alfonso di Ferrara is portrayed in the person of the emperor and Lorenzo de' Medici in that of the accuser.

Apparently because he lost interest (or did not have the time to retain interest) in decorative painting, Raphael left untouched the Holy Trinity frescoes on the ceiling. They were executed by Perugino, Raphael's master and predecessor, between 1507 and 1508.

IV. **The Stanza of Constantine** (1517-1524)

Projected to illustrate the defeat of paganism and the triumph of Christianity, the frescoes in this room continue and complete the political theme of the two preceding rooms. Commissioned by Leo X in 1517, Raphael barely had time to plan the design and decoration before his untimely death, April 6, 1520. The paintings, completed in 1524, were entirely the work of his pupils.

The *Battle at the Milvian Bridge* (today's Ponte Molle) dominates everything in this Stanza: in 312, Constantine opposes and defeats Maxentius. The great crowd of participants in this scene filled with movement is etched as if in classic relief, modelled after Trajan's column; still, everything centers on the majestic, self-assured figure of Constantine. The original design, as we mentioned earlier, was Raphael's; but the somewhat rhetorical style in execution reveals the firmly established personality of Giulio Romano. We detect a strong trace of mannerism, the dominant feature in painting for the next three generations, until the Counter-Reformation.

The *Vision of the Cross*, that the Emperor received as he briefed his troops before the battle, was his personal assurance of victory. The scene faithfully mirrors the details related in the ancient « cohortationes. » The studied, lavish tone – epitomizing mannerism – once again reveals the hand of Giulio Romano. In plain contrast is the deformed dwarf in the foreground – Cardinal de' Medici's jester.

The *Donation of Rome*, probably a collaboration between Giulio Romano and Raffaellino del Colle, recounts the legend of Constantine's gift of temporal power to Pope Silvester I. The power is symbolized by the small statue of the goddess Roma. Vasari claimed to have recognized contemporary artists in this fresco; today's scholars doubt the substance of these claims. At most, they recognize Giulio Romano (raising his hand to his cap) in the figure at the second column on the right.

In the fourth fresco we see the *Baptism of Constantine* in the Lateran baptistery. Pope Silvester bears the features of Clement III. The style of this composition is unlike any other: a hesitant and weak thrust both in design and color recalls the style of Gianfrancesco Penni. The most faithful of Raphael's disciples, he was also the most retiring of the group. To sum up, the frescoes of this Stanza are only a reminder of Raphael's style.

THE DISPUTE ON THE BLESSED SACRAMENT

A – Top section

   1. The Eternal Father
   2. The Word Incarnate
   3. Angels
   4. The Madonna
   5. St. John the Baptist

B – Middle section

   6. St. Peter
   7. Adam
   8. St. John the Evangelist
   9. David
   10. St. Lawrence

11. Jeremiah (?)
12. Angels with the Gospels
13. The Holy Spirit
14. Judas Maccabeus (?)
15. St. Stephen
16. Moses
17. St. James the Lesser
18. Abraham
19. St. Paul

C – Lower section

   20. Blessed Fra' Angelico
   21. Bramante

22. Francesco Maria Della Rovere
23. St. Gregory the Great (features of Julius II)
24. St. Jerome
25. St. Ambrose
26. St. Augustine
27. St. Thomas Aquinas
28. Innocent III
29. St. Bonaventure
30. Sixtus IV
31. Dante
32. Girolamo Savonarola

Raphael Stanzas – Detail of THE DISPUTE ON THE BLESSED SACRAMENT in the STANZA OF THE SIGNATURE: *the Holy Trinity, the Madonna, St. John the Baptist, and four angels with the Gospels.*

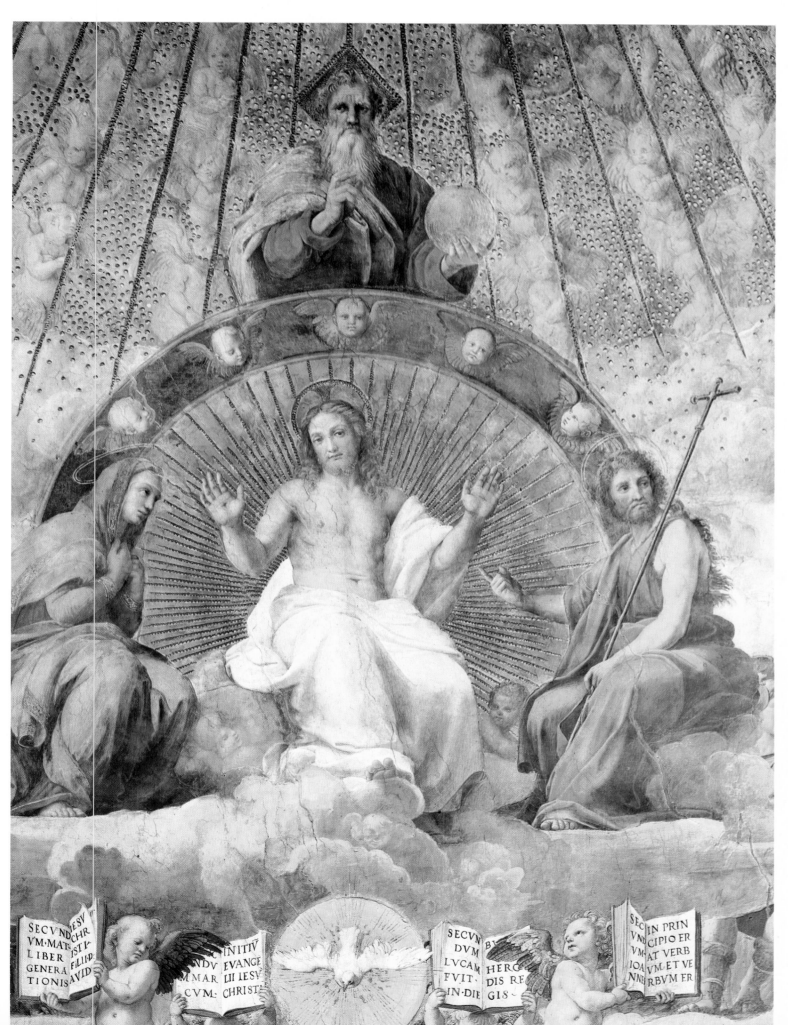

SECVND IESV
VM·MAT· CHR
LIBER ISTI·
GENERA FILII·D
TIONIS·VID

INITIV
NDV EVANGE
MMAR LII IESV
CVM· CHRISTI

SECVN
DVM
LVCAM
FVIT·
IN·DIE

B
HERO
DIS RE
GIS·

SEC IN PRIN
VND CIPIO ER
VM AT VERB
IOA VM·ET·VE
NNE RBVM ER

113

Raphael Stanzas –
THE STANZA OF THE SIGNATURE:
THE DISPUTE ON THE
BLESSED SACRAMENT.   115

Raphael Stanzas – Detail of
THE DISPUTE ON THE BLESSED
SACRAMENT in the Stanza of
the Signature: *group of theologians
among whom are St. Gregory
the Great and St. Jerome.*

116

Raphael Stanzas – Detail of THE DISPUTE ON THE BLESSED SACRAMENT in the STANZA OF THE SIGNATURE: *in the group of theologians are St. Bonaventure, Pope Sixtus IV, Dante and Savonarola.*

118

Raphael Stanzas – Detail of THE DISPUTE ON THE BLESSED
SACRAMENT in the STANZA OF THE SIGNATURE:
portrait of Blessed Fra' Angelico.

Raphael Stanzas – Detail of THE DISPUTE ON THE BLESSED
SACRAMENT in the STANZA OF THE SIGNATURE: *a group of
people among whom are the Blessed Fra' Angelico, Bramante,
and Francesco Maria Della Rovere.*

THE SCHOOL OF ATHENS

1. Plato (Leonardo da Vinci)
2. Aristotle
3. Socrates
4. Xenophanes
5. Eschines (Alcibiades?)
6. Alcibiades (Alexander?)
7. Zeno
8. Epicurus
9. Federico Gonzaga
10. Averroes
11. Pythagoras
12. Francesco Maria Della Rovere
13. Heracleitus (Michelangelo)
14. Diogenes
15. Euclid (Bramante)
16. Zoroaster (Pietro Bembo?)
17. Ptolemy
18. Raphael's self-portrait
19. Portrait of Sodoma

Raphael Stanzas – Detail of THE DISPUTE ON THE BLESSED
SACRAMENT in the STANZA OF THE SIGNATURE: *Dante*.

Raphael Stanzas –
The Stanza of the Signature:
THE SCHOOL OF ATHENS. 125

Raphael Stanzas –
Detail of THE
SCHOOL OF ATHENS
in the STANZA OF THE
SIGNATURE:
Plato and Aristotle.

Raphael Stanzas – Detail of THE SCHOOL OF ATHENS
in the STANZA OF THE SIGNATURE: *Socrates conversing
with Xenophon, Eschines, and Alcibiades.
In the foreground to the left, Averroes,
and Francesco Maria Della Rovere.*

Raphael Stanzas – Detail of THE SCHOOL OF ATHENS
in the STANZA OF THE SIGNATURE: *Heracleitus portrayed*
with *the features of Michelangelo Buonarroti.*

Raphael Stanzas – Detail of THE SCHOOL OF ATHENS
in the STANZA OF THE SIGNATURE:
Zoroaster, Ptolemy, Raphael and Sodoma.

Raphael Stanzas – Detail of THE SCHOOL OF ATHENS
in the STANZA OF THE SIGNATURE: *a group of wise
men, with Diogenes reclining on the steps.*

Raphael Stanzas – THE STANZA OF THE SIGNATURE
THE WALL DEPICTING JUSTICE.
Above, the lunette of the VIRTUES. *On the sides of the
window, the two scenes of* LAW – *(On the base,
the Address of Solon and Moses showing the tablets of the Law).*

132

Raphael Stanzas – THE STANZA OF THE SIGNATURE:
THE WALL DEPICTING JUSTICE. Detail of the fresco of
ST. RAYMOND OF PEÑAFORT PRESENTING THE
DECRETALS TO GREGORY IX.
Gregory IX here has the features of Pope Julius II. 135

Raphael Stanzas – THE WALL DEPICTING JUSTICE
in the STANZA OF THE SIGNATURE: Detail of the
lunette of the VIRTUES: *Temperance*.

MOUNT PARNASSUS

1. Apollo
2. Calliope
3. Terpsicore
4. Erato
5. Polymnia
6. Melpomene
7. Urania
8. Thalia
9. Clio
10. Euterpe
11. Statius
12. Virgil
13. Homer
14. Dante

15. Ennius
16. Anacreon
17. Petrarch
18. Corinna
19. Alcaeus
20. Sappho
21. Ariosto
22. Boccaccio
23. Tibullus
24. Tebaldeo
25. Propertius
26. Ovid
27. Sannazzaro
28. Horace

Raphael Stanzas –
THE STANZA OF THE
SIGNATURE: MOUNT
PARNASSUS. *The
monochrome scenes on the
base depict the Recovery of
the Sibylline Books in the
tomb of Numa; Augustus
Caesar preventing the
destruction of the Aeneid.*

139

Raphael Stanzas – Detail of the PARNASSUS in the STANZA OF THE SIGNATURE: *poets in conversation and Sappho.*

Raphael Stanzas – Detail of the PARNASSUS in the STANZA OF THE SIGNATURE: *a group of poets in conversation, and Horace.*

Raphael Stanzas – The Stanza of the Signature: CEILING.

Raphael Stanzas – Detail of the PARNASSUS in the
Stanza of the Signature: *a group of Muses*.

Raphael Stanzas – Detail of the CEILING in the STANZA OF THE SIGNATURE:
the four medallions depict Philosophy, Theology, Justice and Poetry.

Raphael Stanzas – Detail of THE FREEING
OF ST. PETER in the STANZA OF HELIODORUS:
The angel awakens St. Peter.

146

HELIODORUS PURSUED AND FELLED IN THE TEMPLE

1. The divine messenger
2. Heliodorus
3. The High Priest Onias
4. Pope Julius II
5. Giulio Romano (Raphael?)
6. Marcantonio Raimondi
7. G. Pietro dei Foliarii

Raphael Stanzas –
THE STANZA OF
HELIODORUS:
HELIODORUS
PURSUED AND
FELLED IN
THE TEMPLE
(II MACCABEES,
Chap. III).

Raphael Stanzas – Detail of HELIODORUS PURSUED
AND FELLED IN THE TEMPLE
in the STANZA OF HELIODORUS: *Portrait of Julius II and the
chair-bearers Marcantonio Raimondi and Giulio Romano.*

Raphael Stanzas – Detail of HELIODORUS
PURSUED AND FELLED IN THE TEMPLE
in the STANZA OF HELIODORUS: *the divine
messenger on charger pursues Heliodorus.*

Raphael Stanzas –
THE STANZA OF HELIODORUS:
▼ THE MASS AT BOLSENA.

ST. LEO THE GREAT
CONFRONTS ATTILA

1. Pope Leo X
2. Cardinal Giovanni de' Medici
   (future Leo X)
3. The Master of Ceremonies,
   Paris de' Grassi
4. The Chamberlain, G. Lazzaro
   de' Magistris (called Serapica)
5. St. Peter
6. St. Paul
7. The Colosseum
8. Attila the Hun

Raphael Stanzas – Detail of
THE MASS AT BOLSENA in the
STANZA OF HELIODORUS: *the Swiss Guards.*

Raphael Stanzas –
THE STANZA OF HELIODORUS:
LEO THE GREAT
CONFRONTS ATTILA.

157

Raphael Stanzas – THE STANZA OF HELIODORUS – Detail of
THE MEETING BETWEEN SAINT LEO AND ATTILA:
Portrait of Pope Leo X, and his cortege.

Raphael Stanzas – View of the CEILING of the STANZA OF
HELIODORUS. *The four scenes depict the Burning Bush, the Sacrifice
of Abraham, Noah leaving the Ark, and the Dream of Jacob.*

159

Raphael Stanzas – THE STANZA OF THE BORGO FIRE:
THE BATTLE OF OSTIA.
On the left, Leo X is portrayed in the person of Leo IV.

Raphael Stanzas – THE STANZA OF THE BORGO FIRE:
THE CORONATION OF CHARLEMAGNE.
*(The inscription below reads: Charlemagne,
the sword and the shield of the Roman Church).*

161

Raphael Stanzas –
Detail of THE OATH
OF LEO III in the
Stanza of the
Borgo Fire. *The Pope
is portrayed with the
features of Leo X.
Depicted on the
ornamental front of the
altar is the martyrdom
of St. Catherine
of Alexandria.* 163

Raphael Stanzas –
THE STANZA OF THE
BORGO FIRE:
THE BORGO FIRE.

165

Raphael Stanzas – Detail of THE BORGO FIRE in the
STANZA OF THE BORGO FIRE: *Carrying his father Anchises on his
shoulders, Aeneas flees the city with his son Ascanius.*

Raphael Stanzas – Detail of THE BORGO FIRE in the
STANZA OF THE BORGO FIRE: *Pope Leo IV imparting
his blessing. On the left, the facade of the old St. Peter's Basilica.*

Raphael Stanzas – View of the CEILING in the STANZA OF THE
BORGO FIRE. *The four medallions, the work of his predecessor
Pietro Perugino, were retained by Raphael. They show God the Creator
and angels; Christ between the Baptist and Satan disguised as an old
man; the Holy Trinity and the Apostles; and Christ in glory.*

168

Raphael Stanzas – THE STANZA OF CONSTANTINE:
THE BAPTISM OF CONSTANTINE.

Full view of the CEILING in the STANZA OF CONSTANTINE. *In the center,* THE TRIUMPH OF CHRISTIANITY OVER PAGANISM *painted by Tommaso Siciliano, disciple of Sebastiano del Piombo. The painter was commissioned by Gregory XIII and Sixtus V. The figures on the sides allude to the glory of these two Popes.*

Raphael Stanzas – THE STANZA OF CONSTANTINE: THE CROSS APPEARS TO CONSTANTINE. *Inscribed across the ray of light are the words :* « In this sign you shall conquer. »

MVLTAE·A·CONSTANTINO
MAGNO·ECCLESIAE·IN
EVROPA·AEDIFICATAE
A·QVO·LICINIVS
IN·CRVCIS·SIGNO·VICTVS
SVAE·IN·CHRISTIANOS
IMMANITATIS·POENAS
DEDIT

AVG·ET·TIB·IMPP·CRVCI·SVBICIVNTVR

ANNO·DÑI
MDLXXXV

C·VAL·AVREL·CONSTANTINI
IMP·VICTORIA·QVA·SVBMERSO
MAXENTIO·CRISTIANORVM
OPES·FIRMATAE·SVNT

Raphael Stanzas –
The Stanza
of Constantine:
THE BATTLE
AT THE
MILVIAN BRIDGE. 173

Raphael Stanzas –
THE STANZA OF CONSTANTINE:
THE DONATION OF ROME.
*The inscription reads: « Finally,
Christianity can be freely professed » =
« The donation made by Constantine
to the Church. »*

174

PONT·SVI
PRIMO

THE RAPHAEL LOGGIAS

The Raphael Loggias are unquestionably one of the most representative monuments in the classic Italian Renaissance tradition. When Julius II commissioned Bramante to build a series of superimposed loggias in 1512, he had in mind a facade for the eastern side of the former place of Pope Nicholas III. Bramante continued the work under the reign of Leo X and, when he died, the responsibility for the entire enterprise passed on to Raphael. Vasari writes that Raphael worked « with greater sense of order and decoration, » apparently because he drew more deeply from ancient Roman architecture. Raphael completed the second floor loggia – which is linked with his name – and built still another above it.

Raphael at this time was the official papal architect and also the superintendent general of antiquities. No wonder then that the loggias should reveal so profound an understanding of ancient Roman art. The whole facade structure with its super-imposed loggias clearly evokes the design of such monuments as the Theater of Marcellus and the Colosseum. There too we see the prominent succession of the three orders of columns: the Doric, the Ionic, and the Corinthian. The triple series of arches forms one single series of three open loggias, super-imposed over each other – an ideal passage-way between the Vatican Palace and the panorama of Rome spreading out through the arches.

The Raphael Loggias consist of thirteen arches forming a gallery 65 meters long and 4 meters wide. The pictorial decoration probably was initiated in 1517. The 1513 date, inscribed on the left side of the window in the twelfth arch, probably refers to the beginning of the pontificate of Leo X. In each of the first twelve small arches, Raphael used illustrations inspired by the Old Testament; in the thirteenth, he chose four scenes taken from the New Testament. He probably chose these specific religious subjects in a spirit of competition, challenge – a contest between himself and Michelangelo, between paintings in the Loggias and those completed several years previous in the Sistine Chapel. The 52 scenes on the ceilings of the Loggias are still popularly referred to as « the Raphael Bible. »

The construction of the new St. Peter's Basilica and the paintings in the Stanzas were burden enough, so that Raphael was almost physically unable to take part in the execution of the frescoes in the Loggias. He simply had to be content preparing the design and supervising the actual work. Vasari informs us that there were numerous collaborators. Besides the faithful Gianfrancesco Penni, called « the Craftsman » (il Fattore) and Giulio Romano, the Master called upon Giovanni da Udine – leaving the Venetian workshop of his master, Giorgione – and, in turn, da Udine brought along the Florentine, Perin del Vaga. Polidoro da Caravaggio learned his craft here, starting out as a modest color mixer for the established artists. He was later to establish himself as a foremost decorator of facades in the graffiti style. Other artists of a secondary order swelled the ranks.

Because of the close collaboration of the whole « Raphael School, » it is practically impossible to distinguish the work of one or another particular artist. Though the first impression may suggest talent inferior to Raphael's, his influence and supervision seemed sufficient to reveal a strong cohesion in the pattern, even at the cost of checking the personal development of Penni, Giulio Romano, and Perin del Vaga. All of these, it is certain, were responsible for one or another part of the preparatory drawings.

The independence of Raphael's collaborators is more marked on the walls, decorated in grotesque. They drew their inspiration for this novelty from Roman paintings studied in the ruins of Nero's « Domus Aurea ». The underground ruins were called grottos; hence the name « grotesque. » The Raphael Loggias, however, are not the first example of this imitation of the grotesques. The previous generation of artists had already been attracted by its possibilities. Pinturicchio, Perugino, Filippino Lippi, and Signorelli had already admired and worked in those chandeliers and foliages enlivened by cherubs, birds, bizarre animals, and all kinds of small objects. They enjoyed the free rein for their taste for the playful and fantastic. Of the group, Giovanni da Udine displayed the keenest interest in ancient paintings. Between 1516 and 1519, he reproduced faithful imitations of this style in the decorations of the Stufetta (the bathroom) of Cardinal Bibbiena, and in the small loggia which opens on to the Perrocchetto court (buildings on the third level of the Vatican Palace, now used by the Secretariate of State of the Vatican).

Vasari tells us that Raphael was enormously pleased with his pupil and gave him the reponsibility for the decoration of the rest of the Loggias. Adhering to the Master's over-all plan, Giovanni da Udine designed the painting for the pillars and saw to their execution with the help of collaborators. Unfortunately, this part of the work suffered considerably from exposure to inclement weather. The problem was solved and further deterioration was checked when Pius IX closed the arches in with glass. Still, in many places the paintings are obliterated and the gilding has lost its sheen. In 1952 a fortuitous discovery was made when two half-pillars at the extreme south end of the gallery were exposed after having been walled up since the time of Paul III. We can now admire the sparkling colors of the original work. The paintings have the impression of extraordinary freshness; even the nail holes of the cartoon that guided the artist's hand are visible. These details give an idea of how great the overall beauty must have been.

Unlike the grotesque paintings of the late 15th century, those in the Loggias have a distinctive feature – medallions in stucco atop each pillar. Vasari tells us that Giovanni da Udine was fascinated by the whiteness of the ancient stuccos, particularly those that he found in the Colosseum. After many experiments, he succeeded in rediscovering the formula. The stucco relief work adds immeasurably to the rhythmic pattern of the decoration. Standing out against the colored background of the medallions, the tiny bone white tombs, cameos, coins, suggest details of nature or scenes from every day life. We easily conjure up the vision of the artists at work: one prepares the colors, another applies the stucco to the walls. Again on the keystones of the vaults we spy small figures against the pastel backgrounds – like copies of Greek sculptures. The novelty of the composition is even more striking in the interstices of the arches. Apparently inspired by those in the Colosseum, the figures – without background color of any sort – are white on white. The neo-classic period seems to stand in the wings!

At the base of the inside walls, Perin del Vaga used bronze tones for the chiaroscuro scenes depicting episodes from the Old Testament. Hardly anything is left of this work. An excellent souvenir, however, are the few engraved copies – especially Bartoli's done in the 17th century.

Around this antique style of decoration – enlivened by birds, insects of all kinds, all variety of animals – Giovanni da Udine wove garlands of flowers and fruit. A feeling of cool freshness pervades the Loggias; as if one were in a greenhouse able to look up to see nature around him and the whole panorama of Rome. Reserved exclusively to the Pope, the Loggias used to be lined with ancient statues, like a private museum, where the frescoes reflected the fresh and scholarly classic Greek humanism then in vogue at the court of Leo X.

The Loggias exercised an enormous influence on art. Throughout the whole of the 16th century, artists came to copy the decorative elements in the same way as they copied the ancient Roman monuments in their quest of inspiration for the decoration of private villas. With the advent of the Baroque style in the 17th century, the fashion waned. But it was revived again at the close of the 18th century with the neo-classic period. Catherine II of Russia had an identical loggia built for herself at the Hermitage Palace, pillar for pillar, and with identical decorations on the ceilings. She commissioned the German artist Unterberger to do this work. And so, the echo of the classic monument, Raphael's Loggias, reached almost to the farthest frontiers of the western world.

1.

GOD SEPARATES LIGHT FROM DARKNESS – « When God began to create the heavens and the earth ... said: "Let there be light!". And there was light; and God saw that the light was good. God then separated the light from the darkness » (GENESIS, I 1, 3-4).

2.

GOD SEPARATES EARTH FROM THE WATERS – « Then God said: "Let the waters below the sky be gathered into one place so that the dry land may appear!" ... Then God said: "Let the earth produce vegetation, seed-bearing plants and the various kinds of fruit-trees that bear fruit containing their seed!". And so it was » (GENESIS, I 9, 11).

180

3.

CREATION OF THE
SUN AND MOON –
« *God made the two
great luminaries, the
greater luminary to rule
the day and the smaller
one to rule the night and
the stars also. God set
them in the firmament
of the sky to shed light
on the earth, to rule by
day and by night, and
to separate the light
from the darkness* »
(GENESIS, I 16-18).

4.

CREATION OF THE
ANIMALS – « *Then
God said: " Let the
waters teem with shoals
of living creatures, and
let birds fly over the
earth across the firma-
ment of the sky! " ...
God made the various
kinds of wild beasts of
the earth, the various
kinds of domestic ani-
mals, and all the various
kinds of land reptiles* »
(GENESIS, I 20, 25).

5.

CREATION OF EVE
– « *Then the Lord God had a trance fall upon the man; and when he had gone to sleep, he took one of his ribs, closing up its place with flesh. The rib which he took from the man the Lord God built up into a woman* » (GENESIS, II 21, 22).

6.

ORIGINAL SIN –
« *So when the woman realized that the tree was good for food and attractive to the eye, and further, that the tree was desirable for its gift of wisdom, she took some of its fruit, and ate it; she also gave some to her husband with her, and he ate* » (GENESIS, III 6).

7.

ADAM AND EVE BANISHED FROM EDEN – « *So the Lord God expelled him from the garden of Eden, to till the ground from which he had been taken; he drove the man out, and stationed the cherubim east of the garden of Eden, with the flaming, whirling sword to guard the way to the tree of life* » (Genesis, III 23, 24).

8.

ADAM AND EVE AT WORK – « *So the Lord God said ... to the woman ... : "I will make your pain at child-birth very great"... And to the man he said: "... Cursed shall be the ground through you, in suffering shall you gain your living from it as long as you live ... By the sweat of your brow shall you earn your living ..."* » (Genesis, III 14, 16, 17, 19).

183

9.

BUILDING THE ARK – « *So God said to Noah: "I have resolved on the extermination of all mortals; for the earth is full of wrong-doing through them; I am going to exterminate them from the earth. Make yourself an ark of oleander wood; make the ark with cabins, and smear it with bitumen inside and out ..."* Noah did so; he did just as God had commanded him* » (GENESIS, VI 13, 14, 22).

10.

THE DELUGE – « *Noah, with his sons, his wife, and his sons' wives, went into the ark to escape the waters of the flood ... The flood continued for forty days upon the earth. The waters mounted, and lifted the ark so that it rose above the earth ... Of all that was on the land, everything in whose nostrils was the breath of life died* » (GENESIS, VII 7, 9, 17, 22).

184

11.

LEAVING THE ARK
– « *So that on the seventeenth day of the seventh month the ark grounded on the mountains of Ararat... So Noah came out, his sons, his wife, and his sons' wives accompanying him. Every animal, every reptile, and every bird, everything that moves on the earth came out of the ark by their species* » (GENESIS, VIII 4, 18, 19).

12.

THE SACRIFICE OF NOAH – « *Then Noah built an altar to the Lord, and taking some clean animals and birds of every kind, he offered them as burnt-offerings on the altar ... God then said to Noah and to his sons with him: "As for me, I do hereby establish my covenant with you and your descendants after you"* » (GENESIS, VIII 20; IX 8, 9).

185

13.

ABRAHAM AND MELCHIZEDEK – « *On his return from the defeat of Chedorlaomer and his confederate kings, the king of Sodom came out to the valley of Shaveh ... to meet him, while Melchizedek, king of Salem, brought out bread and wine, and, as priest of God Most High, blessed him, saying: "Blessed be Abram by God Most High"* » (GENESIS, XIV 17-19).

14.

GOD APPEARS TO ABRAHAM – « *After these events the word of the Lord came to Abram in a vision: "Do not be afraid, Abram: I am your shield; your reward shall be very great" ... Then he took him outside, and said: "Now look at the sky, and count the stars if you can". "So shall be your descendants",* he said to him » (GENESIS, XV 1, 5).

186

15.

ABRAHAM AND THREE ANGELS – « *The Lord appeared to him at the terebinth of Mamre ... Raising his eyes, he saw three men standing near him. On seeing them, he ran from the door of his tent to meet them, and bowing to the earth, said: " O sirs, if perchance I find favor with you, please do not pass by without stopping with your servant " »* (GENESIS, XVIII 1-3).

16.

LOT FLEES FROM SODOM – « *When dawn appeared, the angels urged Lot on ... Just as the sun rose over the earth and Lot entered Zoar, the Lord rained sulphur and fire from the sky on Sodom and Gomorrah, devastating those cities and all the valley ... And Lot's wife had looked back, and had become a pillar of salt* « (GENESIS, XIX 15, 23-26).

187

17.

GOD APPEARS TO ISAAC – « *The Lord then appeared to him, and said: "... I will make your descendants as numerous as the stars in the sky, and I will give your descendants this whole country, so that all the nations of the earth will invoke blessing on one another through your descendants"* » (GENESIS, XXVI 2, 4).

18.

ABIMELECH SPIES ON ISAAC – « *When he had been there a long time, Abimelech, king of the Philistines, looked out of his window, and saw Isaac fondling his wife Rebekah. So Abimelech summoned Isaac, and said: "So she really is your wife; then why did you say: 'She is my sister'"?* » (GENESIS, XXVI 8, 9).

19.

ISAAC BLESSES JACOB – « *And taking the best clothes of her older son Esau ... Rebekah dressed her younger son Jacob in them; she put the skins of the kids on his hands and on the smooth parts of his neck. ... Hence Isaac did not detect him, because his hands were hairy, like those of his brother Esau; so he blessed him* » (GENESIS, 15, 16, 23).

20.

ISAAC AND ESAU – « *No sooner had Isaac finished blessing Jacob, indeed Jacob had just left the presence of his father Isaac, when his brother Esau came in from his hunt ... On hearing his father's words, Esau cried loud and bitterly, and said to his father: "Bless me also, my father!"* » (GENESIS, XXVII, 30, 34).

21.

JACOB'S DREAM – *« He had a dream in which he saw a ladder set up on the earth, with its top reaching the sky, and angels of God were ascending and descending on it. Then the Lord stood over him, and said: " I am the Lord, the God of your father Abraham and of Isaac. The land on which you are lying, I am going to give to you and your descendants »* (GENESIS, XXVIII, 12-13).

22.

JACOB MEETS RACHEL – *« While he was still talking ... Rachel arrived with her father's flock ... As soon as Jacob saw Rachel ... Jacob went up, and rolling the stone off the mouth of the well, watered the flock of Laban, his mother's brother. Then Jacob kissed Rachel, and lifted up his voice in weeping »* (GENESIS, XXIX, 9-11).

23.

JACOB REPROVES LABAN – « *So Jacob worked seven years for Rachel ... Then Jacob said to Laban: "Give me my wife; for my time is up "... But in the course of the evening he took his daughter Leah and brought her to Jacob ... Next morning, however, Jacob discovered that it was Leah! So he said to Laban: "... Why then have you cheated me? "»* (GENESIS, XXIX 20, 21, 23, 25).

24.

JACOB RETURNS TO CANAAN – « *So Jacob proceeded to mount his sons and wives on camels, and drove off all his stock, all the live stock which he had acquired ... to go home to his father Isaac in the land of Canaan ... So he fled, with all that belonged to him; starting forth, he crossed the River, and set his face toward the highlands of Gilead* » (GENESIS, XXXI 17, 18, 21).

191

25.

THE DREAMS OF JOSEPH – « *Joseph had a dream, which he told to his brothers, so that they hated him all the more ... Then he had another dream which he recounted to his brothers : " I have just had another dream "*, he said, *" and the sun, moon, and eleven stars made obeisance to me !"*» (GENESIS, XXXVII 5, 9).

26.

JOSEPH SOLD BY HIS BROTHERS – « *As soon as Joseph reached his brothers, they stripped him of his cloak ..., and seizing him, they threw him into the pit ... Some Midianite traders passed by, so pulling Joseph up, they lifted him out of the pit. They sold Joseph to the Ishmaelites for twenty shekels of silver ; and they took him to Egypt* » (GENESIS, XXXVII 23, 24, 28).

192

27.

THE TREACHERY OF POTIPHAR'S WIFE – « *Now Joseph was so handsome and good-looking that some time later the wife of his master took a fancy to Joseph ... One day, however, when he went into the house to do his work ... she caught hold of his coat, saying: "Lie with me!" But he fled, leaving the coat in her hands, and went outdoors* » (GENESIS, XXXIX 6, 11, 12).

28.

THE DREAMS OF THE PHARAOH – « *Joseph said to Pharaoh: "Pharaoh's dream is simple; God would reveal to Pharaoh what he is about to do. The seven fat cows represent seven years, and the seven plump ears represent seven years ... The seven lean and ugly cows that came up after them represent seven years, and so do the seven empty ears blasted by the east wind; there are to be seven years of famine"* » (GENESIS, XLI 25-27).

29.

MOSES SAVED FROM THE WATER – « *Presently Pharaoh's daughter came down to bathe at the Nile, while her maids walked on the bank of the Nile. Then she saw the ark among the reeds and sent her maid to get it* » (EXODUS, II 5).

30.

THE BURNING BUSH – « *While Moses was thending the flock of his father-in-law, Jethro, ... the angel of the Lord appeared to him in a flame of fire, rising out of a bush. .. When the Lord saw that he had turned aside to look at it, God called to him out of the bush. "Moses, Moses!" he said. "Here I am!" said he ... Then Moses hid his face; for he aw afraid to look at God* » (EXODUS, III 1, 2, 4, 6).

194

31

PASSING THROUGH THE RED SEA – « *Then the Lord said to Moses: "Stretch out your hand over the sea, that the water may flow back upon the Egyptians, upon their chariotry and cavalry". So Moses stretched out his hand over the sea ... The water returned, and covered the chariotry and cavalry belonging to the whole army of Pharaoh that had followed them into the sea, not so much as one being left* » (Exodus, XIV 26-28).

32.

THE WATERS RUSHING FROM THE ROCK – « *The Lord said to Moses: "Pass on ahead of the people, taking with you some of the elders of Israel; take the staff in your hand with which you struck the Nile, and go on. I will station myself there before you on the rock at Horeb, and when you strike the rock, water will gush out of it, so that the people may drink"* » (Exodus, XVII 5, 6).

195

33.

MOSES RECEIVES THE TABLETS OF THE LAW – « *The Lord said to Moses: "Ascend the mountain to me, and be present there, that I may give you the stone tablets, with the instructions and commands that I have written on them for their instruction"... So Moses ascended the mountain, while the cloud covered the mountain, and the glory of the Lord rested on Mount Sinai; for six days the cloud covered it* » (EXODUS, XXIV 12, 15, 16).

34.

ADORING THE GOLDEN BULL – « *Moses then turned and descended from the mountain, with the two tablets of the decrees in his hand ... As soon as he came near the camp, he saw the bull and the dancing, whereupon Moses' anger blazed, and he flung the tablets from his hand, and broke them at the foot of the mountain; then he took the bull which they had made, and burned it up* » (EXODUS, XXXII 15, 19, 20).

196

35.

THE COLUMN OF CLOUD – « *Now Moses used to take the tent and pitch it outside the camp ... and as soon as Moses entered the tent, the column of cloud would descend, and stand at the doorway of the tent while he conversed with Moses; and whenever the people saw the column of cloud standing at the doorway of the tent, the people would all rise, and make obeisance, each at the doorway of his tent* » (Exodus, XXXIII 7, 9).

36.

MOSES SHOWS HIS PEOPLE THE TABLETS – « *When Moses descended from Mount Sinai ... Aaron and the Israelites all saw that the skin of Moses' face was in a glow, and they were afraid to approach him. ... After that all the Israelites came up, and he enjoined on them all the things about which the lord had conversed with him on Mount Sinai* » (Exodus, XXXIV 29, 30, 32).

37.

CROSSING THE RIVER – « *When the people left their tents to cross the Jordan ... The priests carrying the ark of the covenant of the Lord took their stand on dry ground, right in the middle of the Jordan, while all Israel crossed over on dry ground, until the whole nation had finished crossing the Jordan* » (JOSHUA, III 14, 17).

38.

THE FALL OF JE-RICHO – « *The seventh time the priests blew the horns, and then Joshua said to the people: "Shout; for the Lord is giving you the city"... So the people shouted, when the horns were blown. As soon as the people heard the sound of the horns, the people raised a mighty shout, and the wall fell flat* » (JOSHUA, VI 16, 20).

39.

JOSHUA STOPS THE SUN – « *It was on the day that the Lord put the Amorites at the mercy of the Israelites that Joshua spoke to the Lord, and in the presence of Israel said: "O sun, stop at Gibeon; and thou moon, at the valley of Aijalon!" So the sun came to a stop, and the moon stood still, until the nation took vengeance on their foes* » (JOSHUA, X 12-13).

40.

DIVIDING THE PROMISED LAND – « *Then the whole Israelite community assembled at Shiloh, and set up the tent of meeting there, the region having been brought into subjection to them ... So Joshua cast lots for them at Shiloh before the Lord; and there Joshua distributed the land among the Israelites, to each his share* » (JOSHUA, XVIII 1, 10).

199

41.

SAMUEL ANOINTS DAVID KING – « Samuel ... purified Jesse and his sons and invited them to the sacrifice ... "Are these all the young men?" Samuel said to Jesse. "There is still the youngest", he said, "but just now he is shepherding the flock". So he sent and brought him in. Now he was ruddy, a youth with beautiful eyes and attractive appearance ... then Samuel took the horn of oil and anointed him in the midst of his brothers, (I SAMUEL, XVI 4, 5 11-13).

42.

DAVID SLAYS GOLIATH – « Now when the Philistine arose and came and drew near to meet David ... David put his hand in his bag and took from it a stone and slung it and it struck the Philistine on his forehead; and the stone sank into his forehead, so that he fell on his face to the earth » (I SAMUEL, XVII 48-49).

43.

THE TRIUMPH OF DAVID – « *Then David defeated Hadadezer, the son of Rehob, the king of Zobah … and David took from him a thousand chariots, seven thousand cavalry, and twenty thousand infantry … So David won fame. On his return, he overcame eighteen thousand Edomites in the valley of Salt* » (II SAMUEL, VIII 3, 4, 13).

44.

DAVID AND BATH-SHEBA – « *Then one day at sunset, David got up from his couch, and walked to and fro upon the roof of the king's house; and from the roof he saw a woman bathing. The woman was very beautiful … So David sent messengers and took her; and she came to him, and he lay with her* » (II SAMUEL, XI 2, 4).

45.

SOLOMON CON-
SECRATED KING –
« *Accordingly Zadok the
priest, and Nathan the
prophet, and Benaiah,
the son of Jehoiada, to-
gether with the Chere-
thites and the Pelethites,
caused Solomon to ride
on the mule of King Da-
vid, and brought him to
Gihon. Then Zadok the
priest took a horn of
oil from the tent and
anointed Solomon* »
(I KINGS, I 38-39).

46.

THE JUDGMENT
OF SOLOMON –
« *Then two women of
ill fame came to the
king ... Then the king
said: "This one dec-
lares, 'This is my child,
the living one, and your
child is dead'. And the
other declares, 'No; but
your son is the dead and
my son is the living!'.
'Get me a sword', said
the king ... 'Cut the
living child in two'..."* »

(I KINGS, III 16, 23-25).

47.

THE QUEEN OF SHEBA – « *Now when the queen of Sheba heard of the fame of Solomon through the name of the Lord, she came to test him with hard questions. So she came to Jerusalem with a very large retinue, with camels bearing spices and very much gold and precious stones; and when she came to Solomon, she conversed with him about all that was in her mind* » (I KINGS, X 1-2).

48.

CONSTRUCTING THE TEMPLE – « *As for the house which King Solomon built for the Lord, its length was sixty cubits, its breadth twenty cubits, and its height thirty ... In the fourth year was the foundation of the house of the Lord laid, in the month Ziv ... Thus he was seven years in building it* » (I KINGS, VI 2, 37, 38).

203

49.

THE BIRTH OF CHRIST – « *And Joseph went up from Galilee from the town of Nazareth to Judea to the city of David called Bethlehem... While they were there, the time came for her child to be born, and she gave birth to her first-born son; and she wrapped him up, and laid him in a manger, fot there was no room for them at the inn* » (LUKE, II 4, 6, 7).

50.

THE EPIPHANY OF CHRIST – « *Now after the birth of Jesus at Bethlehem ... astrologers from the east arrived at Jerusalem, and asked: "Where is the newly born king of the Jews?" ... And they went into the house and saw him with his mother, Mary, and they threw themselves down and did homage to him. They opened their treasure boxes and presented the child with gifts of gold, frankincense, and myrrh* » (MATTHEW, II 1, 2, 11).

51.

THE BAPTISM OF CHRIST – « *Then Jesus came from Galilee to the Jordan, to John, to be baptized by him ... And when Jesus was baptized, he went right up out of the water, and the heavens opened, and he saw the Spirit of God come down like a dove and light upon him, and a voice from heaven said: "This is my Son, my Beloved! this is my Chosen"* » (MATTHEW, III 13, 16, 17).

52.

THE LAST SUPPER – « *When evening came, he took his place at table with the twelve disciples. ... As they were eating Jesus took a loaf and blessed it, and he broke it in pieces and gave it to his disciples, saying: "Take this and eat it. It is my body!" And he took the wine-cup and gave thanks and gave it to them, saying: "You must all drink from it ... "* » (MATTHEW, XXVI 20, 26, 27).